Hock City

A Story by

C. Schmidt

SLEEK PUBLISHING GROUP | Maryland

Copyright © 2018 by C. Schmidt

Contact

Email: scholarman@gmail.com

Phone: 301-842-4326

www.scholarman.com

Instagram: @scholarman

Twitter: @scholarman

Facebook: ScholarManMusic

ISBN:

Cover Design by: Local Summer Co | http://www.localsummerco.com

To the Creator of the universe –

Thank you for the opportunity.

Table of Contents

Get rid of them all. Take them as far away as you can, without causing suspicion to those in the city.

Entry Point

The thickness of the air cut through the vegetation throughout the hills. Heatwaves distorted the view of tumbleweed on the terrain from afar. A rattle snake slithered in the distance, while Jackrabbits nibbled on shrubbery, with a close eye on the predators near. Scorpions moved quickly along foliated rock.

Vultures circled and landed on light posts. They pecked at one another at times, clashing in regard to whom had dibs on what laid below. Others waited patiently, gawking at random intervals.

A middle-aged man lied in between weathered trees and cacti. The cacti stood watch between the sun and the valleys. The wind blew through his hospital gown, while dust was on his face, seemingly embedded in his five o'clock shadow.

A young kid in oversized slacks and suspenders noticed the man, and approached with caution; after a brief once-over he kneeled beside him. He poked the body of the man with a stick but received no response. The boy removed his fedora, and put his ear to the man's chest; the man was breathing at a steady, slow pace - but this was no place for a nap. He shook him, since the man was alive.

"Hey mister, you okay? Mister!" He shoved him with force.

After another shove, the disoriented man let out a hard, loud cough - causing the kid to jump to his feet. The man squinted his eyes as he opened them slowly. The dust debris from the environment created a sticky residue around his eyelids. His vision was blurred momentarily; blinded by long, bright rays that stretched from every corner of his sight. He was soaked in sweat; vomit covered the pebbled ground next to him. His hospital gown was soiled.

He laid motionless; the only movement was in his mind. Thoughts that circled like the vultures above. He bent one leg and held his hand over his eyes to block the brightness. The wind blew sporadically, but not enough to cool him. The salt from his perspiration irritated his eyes, as he strained to see the small person next to him. At first he only saw the silhouette of the kid.

"Mister, are you okay? Need help? Man, you don't look good. Why you out here like this? You better get up before you get a heat stroke! Them birds up there gon' get you."

The kid had a quick tongue, as if his mind was several steps ahead of his words. A race the two ran often.

He pulled on the man's hand to help him rise to a seated position. Once on his backside, he looked around and studied his surroundings. His face and hair was dirty, while his lips were chapped. His back ailed from laying on the hard unleveled ground for some time. His head pounded like he had been thrown against a brick wall.

His anxiety grew as his mind danced around various thoughts. He had unconsciously been in this spot for quite a while. To the vultures, he was near death and a new option on the menu.

How he managed to survive in this remote location, and in this condition, both of which left him dumbfounded.

"Do you have water?" he asked. He cringed after the question, as his pain worsened. He spat sand fragments from his mouth, and then grabbed his side, near his lower abdomen. His muscles cramped due to his dehydration. They felt stiff like an old, dry sponge.

"A little. Clean water is hard to come by in these parts." The boy pulled out a flask, unscrewing the top. The dehydrated man grabbed the flask in haste before it was offered to him. Water splashed from the nozzle during the exchange, frustrating the man. He sucked his teeth as he realized that every drop was priceless. He took one last big gulp, while cherishing the taste.

"Where am I? Who are you?"

The young boy, with one hand in his pocket, kicked rocks and then pointed towards a group of buildings, far in the distance, "You near Hock City sir. Pineville, actually. This area is Pineville. Name's Jesse. What's ya' name?"

The man's eyes widened. *How did I get here?* He pondered. He look at the hospital gown he wore; then, he looked at the area around him, perturbed. He stood to his feet, dusted off his arms and legs, and tied the gown tight around his body to cover his buttocks. He started to walk toward buildings he could see. They were faint in the horizon.

He looked around as he walked, silently searching for clues as to how he got where he was. The land was like an optical illusion. He looked at the light poles near, including the hills and the roads. Every time he felt like he was gaining ground, he was misled. His parched state and skewed imagination began to get the best of him.

His instincts led, and the kid followed.

Pineville

Why am I in this gown?

The sun started to retreat and the air cooled after walking for a while. The man came to what appeared to be a residential area. Intersections, stop signs, fences; inoperable stoplights. Pineville looked as if it stretched several miles in every direction, as far as his eyes could see.

He stood and observed his surroundings. Pineville was not a pretty place from what it seemed. The air around the area smelled chaotic. The remnants of bad hygiene, smoke, sex and overall mayhem swarmed the area. It was a cesspool.

The streets and remnants of the neighborhoods were dilapidated. Signs were smeared with bullet holes with the remains of what looked like dried blood. Mounds of sand covered the bones of decayed homes. Shreds of torn advertisements hung on light poles.

The man vomited at his first encounter of excrement, which smothered part of cracked sidewalks and chipped asphalt. He didn't have much vomit to purge due to his dehydration. Nonetheless, the smell of yesterday's waste turned his stomach. It was as if people defecated and threw waste wherever (and whenever).

He looked upon the landscape with unpleasant awe and uncertainty.

"What's your name, sir?" Jesse asked again. He walked closely and stared at the man, eager to get an answer. He admired his watch as it glistened from the sunlight with each swing of his arm.

"Langston."

"Nice to make your acquaintance, Mr. Langston. That's a nice timepiece you got there."

"Thanks." Langston looked at the watch, puzzled. It was the only thing he wore, outside of the hospital gown. He smiled with his eyes because the watch was a gift. It was something that he possessed since he was a child.

"Where am I? What is this place?" Langston asked.

"Right now, you in Pineville or the 'Pines,' as we call it. That way takes you to Hock City. It's the best place ever, well for me anyways. I ain't never been nowhere else. I come out here to find anything worth taking back. For lines and all."

"The Pines," Langston repeated to gauge his recollection.

"Yeah, Pineville."

Jesse pointed to the entrance sign for the area. Graffiti and other markings covered most of what was left. *The Pines. Find your light.* Tall, lean people with rods were drawn on a portion of the wall.

"You have never been beyond this city?"

"No, sir."

"Why not?"

"Don't know. There really ain't no other place to go. Where you from, mister?"

Langston's thoughts raced again. It was a challenge for him to narrow them down. Various visuals continued to flash in his mind. He couldn't remember much, such as how he got to this place. The desert, the gown.

Langston's eyes wandered again. He didn't recognize anyone.

They continued to walk.

Darkness began to fall as they grew closer to the walls of Hock City; new faces emerged. Langston saw no one that looked familiar. Most of the people appeared to be scavengers. They looked for items that they could use or barter. Cheerless, focused facial expressions.

They all wore the same outfits with small modifications. Some wore extra clothing underneath like a sweater, jacket or shirt. It provided warmth for the cold climate at night. They carried book bags and trash bags full of their belongings, while using makeshift wagons for transport. These people fought each other often, because everyone needed something. Sometimes stealing was the only way to get what was needed.

Langston and Jesse arrived at a gas station. A malfunctioning, cracked logo was in front of it. A robot drinking a cola was displayed in an ad, hanging in the window. Langston noticed another sign dangling, spinning between 'closed' and 'open' due to the short, sporadic bursts of wind. The movement of the sign generated a constant, fluttering sound. Crows, on the roof – cawed. The sound of the birds alerted Langston.

"I'm going to stop here. Maybe someone in there can help – tell me how to get home."

Langston looked toward the station. Jesse walked in the other direction as Langston continue to walk toward it. He stopped for a moment and then looked back in a concerned fashion. He picked up a rock and threw it at cans on the ground. The crows, startled at the sound, widened their wings.

Jesse paused before speaking, "Oh. Okay, Mr. Langston; I will see ya' later I guess. If you need anything, just look for me here." He jogged back towards Langston to hand him a faded, worn flyer that he pulled from his pocket. It was partially unreadable. Langston did his best to decipher the words.

C'mon by -- Pearl's Cas --o and Girls! XXX Bet---en 777 P----- and Nor-- -- amond Drive.

"Why is a kid – like you- at a joint like this?"

Jesse couldn't have been no more than thirteen or fourteen years old. He had a young face with a voice that was light and crackled at times. His skin was golden like the sun, right before setting. He had peach fuzz around his mouth and chin, as well as curly hair and oversized clothes.

"Madam Pearl got the only place with food, clean water and a place to rest my head. Well, there is also Guardian's Grove, but only big line folk can go there. I only heard about that place. I ain't never been."

"As long as I do what Madam Pearl tells me to do, I can stay with her for free. She takes care of me and some others. It's better inside those walls then out here. Trust me, you don't want to be out here in the dark. Remember those people you saw on that sign? They come out sometimes. And you don't want to be out here when they do. Anyways, I best keep moving. See you around, I guess."

Jesse picked up his pace, and continued in the direction of Hock City.

Langston thought about what he was told: *Guardian's Grove. Sounds like a place with answers.*

He watched as Jesse maneuvered the Pines, greeting various people he passed, waving at times. He moved like a politician, desperate for that last vote, but with the cool to not show it.

Most of the people looked at him with a despondent expression, keeping their business while scavenging. Some shewed him away. Other swarmed him to see what goods he had found. No matter what was going on, the exchange of goods was the top priority when Jesse was around.

Langston was surprised at Jesse's confidence. He watched him travel alone in what seemed to be an unsafe environment for a child.

Just the facial expressions on some of these people were creepy; Jesse stood in the midst of it all. The other children seemed to be attached to adults by the hip, even protected. But Jesse operated like an adult, or at least with the respect of one.

The area in which he stood was miles away from the walls of Hock City. Miles away from better living, or so it seemed. A place only some people could visit. The others – well - they could only dream of getting inside the walls.

Outcasts.

The Man with the Scar

Langston took time to gather himself. He was hugged by the desert atmosphere. The dry air that filled his lungs left him feeling just as woozy as it did when he awoke. But the cooler temperature soften the blow, as daylight subsided in the desert.

He needed nourishment before his body started to eat him alive from the inside. His stomach knotted and tightened like a snake's coil. He was barely moving on fumes. He stood for a moment, looking into the depths of the desert and the Pines. He took a deep breath, relaxing the pain moving inside him.

Sluggish, he continued toward the gas station where he looked inside. *Tire & lube services available* a metallic sign read above the door, which hung behind the counter. More advertisements, for cigarettes and candies, were displayed on an adjacent wall.

The grime on the building was thick, so much that it was a challenge to see inside. Unkempt grass grew rampant in several areas on the pavement. A rusty gutter spout rattled, as it tapped the side of the building. What was left of a torn recliner, with the cotton from the cushions exposed, sat near the front door beside a tobacco spit-jar.

Unleaded gas read as seven dollars and some change a gallon, posted on a tall sign at the edge of the station lot. The price remained, even though there wasn't a running car in sight.

The roads were mostly gravel and chunks of broken concrete; aged with fading lines. The only cars Langston saw were piled up on the side and in the rear of the station. It appeared that this station became a scrap yard - full of decrepit and abandoned cars.

He grabbed the door of the station to open it; it swung open without much help. He continued to observe the remains of what appeared to be a once thriving business.

The shelves were empty, with the exception of depleted bottles of liquor, toiletries – rotten apples and molded bread. 'Schmick's, sliced thick.' Dust was now the new hot item. Large bugs scattered in the darkest corners of the room. Another set hovered in the air in front of him. A bird flew out of a crack in the wall. The mild light from the sun setting, pierced through this crack, providing the only real lighting in the room, due to the grime that covered the windows.

He stepped on broken glass as he moved around. The sound betrayed him.

"Don't move another fucking step," said a voice, with a pause between every other word. The voice was calm and manly; gravely but at a whisper.

Langston put his hands up near his shoulders as slow as he could. He trembled as he felt unstable on the scattered glass, which slid with each of his steps – piercing the bottom of his feet.

"Turn around slow...and I mean slow, dammit," the voice spoke again.

"I don't want any trouble, friend. I'm just looking for -" Langston's voice shivered.

"I ain't your friend, and I don't give a squirrel's left nut what you looking for *wanderer*," the voice cut him off with a mild but fierce tone.

Langston turned around slightly to face the voice head on during the brief exchange. Almost instantaneously, a 12-guage double-barrel shotgun appeared out of the dark through the ray of light that shined through the cracks in the wall.

Before Langston could turn around completely, the mystery man put the barrels at the tip of his nose. He was already weak from the lack of food and water. Now his legs felt like they would give way, as he felt the coolness of the barrels on his skin. He grew even more wobbly. If he had any fluid in his bladder he would have pissed himself.

"Sir, please -- I promise you I am not a threat. I just need help. Food if you got any. You can frisk me if you want. I don't have anything on me. Look, all I have on is this gown. What could I possibly hide?" he pleaded as he continued to turn around, proving he was not armed.

A man emerged out the dimness. His stark-white beard entered the light first. Then, a long, thick scar that covered his right eyebrow and eye was visible. He stood a foot taller than Langston's six-foot-one frame, with a wide masculine neck and prominent jawline. He wore a trench coat that was missing the sleeves. His arms and hands were massive.

A long rectangular line was tattooed on each of his arms, with smaller designs inside various blocks. They stretched from the peak of his shoulders down to the top of his wrists. His demeanor was intense and his stature was colossal.

"Why you here? What you want, boy? I could kill you right now for trespassin.'"

"Please - don't. I just…I just need some food and water. Clothes if you got any. Answers." Langston spoke with his eyes just as much as his mouth. He didn't break eye contact. His life depended on this. He moved his fingers in correlation to his words while he spoke, but kept perfectly still otherwise. He then put his hands down, so that he could lean on the counter next to him. He was famished; his feet were starting to bleed from the glass.

"I ain't say you could put ya' damn hands down." The man moved his gun upward with a brisk motion.

Langston put his hands back up but higher, causing his hospital gown to rise. He didn't know what to expect next.

The man with the scar never changed his tone of voice. He instilled fear, even with his quiet and calm demeanor. He stepped closer to Langston and examined his appearance.

"I would check you for weapons, but you're right. It don't look like you have anywhere to hide anything - except for one place. I have no plans on checking there." He inhaled the sweaty mess that Langston had become, as a result from being in the desert for some time. "Mmm. You don't smell like anyone from 'round here."

Langston looked at the man with a confused expression, shook his head and then gazed at the floor. His dehydration grew in severity.

"Water is like gold here, so that means we don't bathe much. Most of the people outside them walls smell like shit. But you - - you smell like a fresh basket of fruit, pretty boy," the man with the scar continued. He pulled the hammers back on the shotgun.

The hammers engaging was enough for Langston to fall to his knees and pass out.

You Trespassin'

The man with the scar shook his head in frustration while he lifted Langston's limp body from the station floor. He put one of his arms over his shoulder and dragged him to the back of the building, down a narrow hallway toward another room.

The walls were brown and dusty, with vintage photos displayed, mostly of Pineville and Hock City. The photos portrayed Pineville before it became overrun by poverty and degradation. Lush green grounds, massive trees, smiles and mostly - peace.

Hock City before the greed, the segregating, the gambling and the killing. Fancy cars, clothing and thriving businesses. Everyone looked wealthy or well off: there were all types of people, all types of personalities.

He slid one of the pictures on the wall to the left and an adjacent wall opened. He put Langston down on the floor, turned around and walked backwards - lugging him into the room, through the narrow opening.

He leaned his gun against the wall beside his cot, in the same place underneath a dim Betty Cage light. One that flickered with the slightest movement. He dropped Langston on a similar cot positioned against the opposite wall. He smacked Langston's face to wake him after cleaning the wounds on his feet and giving him some time to rest.

"Wake up! Hey! Boy! Wake up! I gots something for ya.'"

Langston didn't budge at first. The man with the scar tried again by banging on the outside of an old pot. Langston struggled to open his eyes. He blinked a few times, only to see a fuzzy display of a worn ceiling filled with watermarks and holes. He rolled onto one of his shoulders and then sat up using his elbow as a crutch. He leaned forward and rested on his legs, while rubbing his face.

"Here," the man with the scar threw a hooded shirt and pants at Langston, "Put those on; I'm tired of seeing your bare ass. I found an old pair of shoes out back. They may not fit perfectly, but they will do. Better shake 'em, though. Might have a visitor or two inside of 'em."

"Where am I?"

The man with the scar sat on the edge of his cot. He grabbed his gun and put it across his lap with the barrel pointed slightly in the direction of Langston. Then, he corked the top of a dark, round jug. Taking a long swallow of the contents, he belched and then held the jug outward toward Langston.

Langston's gaze was drawn to the darkness of the barrels. He daydreamed for a moment before taking the jug and drinking a big portion of it himself. The strong, salty liquid splashed on his face and clothing due to his anxiousness.

"Argh! What is that?" Langston complained. He spat the remaining liquid from his mouth, then used his shirt sleeve to wipe his face. The liquid doused the man with the scar, covering parts of his hands and gun. An act that brought him great annoyance.

"Hmph. You's in no position to be picky, pretty boy," he said. He wiped his hands and gun with an old cloth. "That there's an ale I brew myself. The *finest* between here and Hock." He spoke with conviction.

"Shit - that's horrible," Langston said without hesitation.

The man with the scar gave Langston a hard stare. The stare was just as assertive as his whisper. It was as if his eyes could break away from his face and walk freely. They came to bully Langston's soul.

The man with the scar caressed the handle of the shotgun.

"Sorry, sorry, sorry! It's great, really…" Langston spoke with regret.

The man took his gaze away and scooted back on his cot, in effort to rest his back on the wall.

"So…are you going to tell me who you are? Where I am?" Langston asked as he changed into the clothes of which the man with the scar provided.

"My name isn't important. What's important is why you tresspassin.'"

"Didn't realize where I was. Just came here hoping for help. I woke up not too far from here in the desert. I have no idea how I got there. Or why I was in that gown. Jesse, a kid…found me up the road. I saw this place, and figured someone could help. My name is Langston."

He reached out for a handshake as Langston finished his explanation. The man with the scar didn't oblige. Instead, he folded his arms, crossed his ankles and then responded.

"Hmph. That kid. Always stumbling on shit he shouldn't. One of these days. One of these days."

"Well, nice to meet you – um, *sir*; since you won't tell me what your name is. Thanks for the ale. But I need to know how I got here. Can you tell me anything that can help me? Point me to who can?"

The man with the scar turned his stare away. He rubbed his hands slowly as he pondered. The veins in his hands were like snakes - buried beneath his rough, dry skin. The arid climate was often harsh on the body; lotion was a hard item to find. His knuckles were large like miniature mountains, trapped under sand.

"Can't be too much help. All I know is these station walls. Out there, you on your own. Follow them raggedy signs to get wherever you going. Maybe that kid can help you more."

Langston listened to the man's comments and thought more about his whereabouts. He twirled his thumbs and looked to the side. *What did I see when I awoke?*

"C'mon man, give me something. All I remember is desert everywhere: a bunch of cactuses, dirt and hills, as well as old street signs. Just desert. Nothing else. Oh, um - and light poles. Yeah, light poles."

"Light poles…, with vultures nearby?"

"Yeah."

"Them light poles are the only ones left standing for some reason. But that's all I know. They don't work."

"Nothing else you can tell me?"

As the man with the scar spoke, he reached over toward a small nightstand to the right of his cot. He opened the wooden door on the front, reached in and pulled out a thin scrapbook from the shelf. The book was made of dark, worn leather. A feather hung from the inside with a string and beads attached. He wiped the cover clean of dust.

"I found this book in the ole Woodson sto.' Wasn't much left of that place. That bastard destroyed Pineville. Destroyed Hock. Sucked us dry. Fucker."

"Us who? What is that?"

"Us, the people. The citizens. The people that have kept this place what it is. Alive and kicking. I've been using this book to keep the latest happenins'."

"The latest *happenings*?"

"Mmm hmm. You ain't the first wanderer."

"Wanderer?"

"You gon' repeat everything I say? Yeah, *Wanderer*," Kinth responded, visibly frustrated. He looked at the front of the book with an expression of familiarity. His mild arthritis was evident as he opened the front flap. "Time to time wanderers come by here, but not often. I reckon they all seek the same answers. Normally they take one look at this station and keep walking. They all have the same look on their face."

"What look?"

"That one right there," the man with the scar said as he nodded toward Langston. "The ones that don't come by here, the vultures get. Either that or the Desert Dwellers get 'em."

"Vultures I get, but Desert Dwellers? What, like - people that live out here, in this wilderness? You speak of them like they, like they - some other species of people or something. Can't be real."

"Oh - it's real, pretty boy. As real as I'm sitting here speaking to you. Doesn't make a difference what you think is real or not. I seen what I seen."

"So...what do these *Desert Dwellers* do?" Langston made air-quotes with his fingers, "They eat them?"

"Eat 'em, kill 'em, whatever. One in the same. Normally that kid, or someone else, finds 'em already dead. Sometimes the Dwellers take them away. You got lucky. You got *real* lucky."

"And then...then what? He takes whatever he finds and sells it?"

"You not as dense as you look, boy. You might just survive this place."

"But how did these people end up here? The people you spoke of. Out here in this place?"

The man with the scar either ignored the question or he didn't hear it. The man continued to explore his book as Langston spoke. He turned to a page that contained a list. The list was simple in structure. It was a ledger, which listed various traits of the different people that stopped by the station. Things such as height, gender and other physical attributes. Any details he could remember.

'Female, average height, light-colored.

Male, tall, brown, no shoes.

Female, dark, tattoo.'

"All these people had one common thing about them."

"Which was what?"

"Isn't it obvious? That they didn't know how they got here. It was like they were dropped outta nowhere."

Langston closed his eyes as he lied down on the bed. He tried his best to remember the events that led up to where he was now, including why he was in a hospital gown, but his mind drew a blank. He smacked his head out of exasperation.

"Shit!"

"Mmm. Well, I told you all I know. I'm hittin' the sack. There's more ale in that jug right there. All I got. Don't waste it. Either drink it or leave it. Take what you need and be on yo' way by sun-up."

A defeated Langston looked at him. The man with the scar turned over in his cot to go to sleep. He rolled over without a care; unenthused to say the least. Langston figured that he had done this song and dance one too many times.

Highway 99

Langston moved around on the cot uncontrollably. He dozed a few times, but couldn't get comfortable, partly because of body aches and pains. His muscles were weak, and the thin cot didn't help. Nor did the odd insects that circled the room.

He didn't know what was worse - the hard desert ground or his new sleeping arrangements. The cot hadn't any back support, while the potato sack was filled with sand for a pillow. It definitely wasn't pleasant, but at least he was indoors, away from vultures and the Desert Dwellers.

Yeah, okay. Desert Dwellers. He chuckled at the thought.

He grew tired of staring at the ceiling while hearing rodents and other disturbing sounds. The man with the scar's farts and belching throughout the night was no picnic, either. He decided to leave. It had to be in the wee hours of the morning because of the darkness across the land.

He grabbed a jug of ale and an empty potato sack in which to carry it, heading toward the front of the station. He walked as carefully as he could, so that he wouldn't wake the man with the scar. He didn't seem like the type that enjoyed interrupted sleep.

He stood for a moment at the station's entrance, looking out the soiled windows. He rubbed one spot of the window hard enough to create an eyehole. There was little lighting except the stars above the old station. A glow shone from the lights in the main section of Hock City within the distance behind the walls. But getting there seemed like a task. The station was miles away, and the darkness didn't seem friendly. Quite unfriendly, in fact, if you looked at it long enough.

He regained some strength, and was awake. He might as well try to make his way there; friendly or not, he had to keep going.

He walked with caution along the remains of the roads within Pineville. He practically tip-toed. He sipped on the ale whenever necessary. It was growing on him but what choice did he have? He noticed a road mark: Highway 99. It hung on its last screw, squeaking as it swung momentarily.

The road looked hopeless behind him, as if it led nowhere. Possibilities and answers were in front of him. He looked around cautiously, while doing his best not to make any noise. With every step, the glow of lights in front of him grew larger of which were compelling to look at it in the moment.

The journey was taxing at night, but not as bad as during the day. The lack of sun meant less heat, and less heat made it easier to travel - but only if you were prepared for the temperature change.

Looking out into the desert, though, was troubling - as if looking out into deep ocean water while submerged. What was lurking? Paranoia. Langston tried not to look to the sides, but rather only toward what was in front of him. Lights.

He grew fidgety with the journey; his nervousness heightened. A flock of crows cawed without warning, taking flight in his peripheral vision. *More crows.* They previously fed on the remains of a wild hare, which lied on the side of the road. All that remained of the hare was fragments of dark, reddish meat, wrapped around cracked bones and shredded organs.

The sound of the crows startled him, causing him to run. He tripped and fell, due to the oversized pants he wore. During his tumble, the jug of ale slipped from his fingers. It shattered when it hit the ground. The ale oozed from the cracked jug and engulfed a portion of the asphalt.

Through the liquid he could see the reflection of the stars in the sky, as well as the sun. The sun still had a dark orange glow, but it was not bright enough to light the land. He also noticed his face, touching his cheeks with his fingertips. He sat at the edge of the sand to gather himself. His reflection and the stars were the only things that seemed normal in the last few hours.

He clinched his fists out of exasperation. He wondered where he would be able to find drinkable water.

Suddenly, a deep whistling sound crept into his ears. The wind began to rip faster and heavier. The pressure from the wind dove deeper onto his chest. It caused the earth to tremble. The ground shook beneath him. Gravel moved quickly across his path. The wind and sand continued to stir, and then a loud snap of thunder rang throughout the Pines. The brightness briefly covered the sky.

He looked around but saw nothing at first. He was concerned about what was occurring, but he continued to examine his leg. It felt strained from the fall. He cuffed the pants that he wore and then he swiftly jumped to his feet. He peered into the darkness. He could see glowing circles in the distance with each strike of lightening. One set appeared at first; a rattling sound followed.

"Jesse, is that you?" The circles were low to the ground but grew larger and higher with the longer he stared. Then, another set appeared along with another, and then many more. He realized that the circles weren't just circles. They were eyes. They were auburn in color with jagged lines that resembled tree branches. The branches moved as the eyes moved.

"Oh, shit!" Langston didn't hang around to get a closer look. He took off, running in the opposite direction. Quickly he remembered that his right leg was injured. He slowed his pace while he grumbled in agony. He wasn't able to gain much ground.

The more eyes he saw the more he moved. He felt defenseless and surrounded. The noise which surrounded him became louder. It was a combination of wind and a chant.

"Woooo-heeeee! Woooo-heeeee! Woooo-heeeee!"

He pushed through his anguish and hobbled faster, despite the fear tearing at his soul. Heavy-breathing and more swears followed. He looked over his shoulder to ensure whatever was lurking around him was no longer near. He was elevated into the air at this moment, and then thrown backwards.

A gush of an enormous and powerful wind consumed him. His sluggish body hit the ground near two soiled, deserted aluminum trashcans. He grabbed his head in agony, got up on one knee, and then grabbed the lid to one of the cans. He placed it in front of him as a shield. The he began to wield it, while hoping to hit whatever the force was in front of him. To his relief, a broken bottle was also near and under a pile of disposed food. He bravely utilized it as a knife, for it was the only form of a weapon within his reach.

"Who's there? Huh? What the hell do you want?! Huh?! Come out! I ain't scared! C'mon!" he yelled as he swung the bottle in the darkness.

As he looked around, he could also see small fires scattered throughout homes in the Pines. Each flame was quickly extinguished, after the commotion. The shadows of people scattering, filled each dwelling.

"Oh! So nobody gon' help?!"

His windpipe started to close, as a pressure formed around his neck and then his arms. His body was being squeezed, but he couldn't see anything on him. He yanked and moved as much as he could to break free. The pressure forced him to drop the bottle, and then the trashcan lid was snatched from his fingers. Slowly, sand particles began to form into a person.

Long, lanky arms formed, as he was being held in a bear hug from behind. Another arm with a hand attached, immobilized him by the throat. His windpipe further consumed; oxygen became minimal. All of this happened with the same set of eyes around him. His fear grew. His eyes widened. He tried his best to break free but to no luck. His breath began to escape him.

As sweat rolled down his face, Langston's eyes enlarged more. He tried his best to break free but to no luck. His breath began to escape him, the more he struggled to break free.

The particles completed their transformation. Once completed, Langston couldn't believe what he saw. Before him stood multiple beings - creatures. They were tall with body markings. Eight feet in height, some taller. *Desert Dwellers!* he thought, as his eyes began to focus on what stood before him.

He still managed to squeeze out words, even with the tight grasp around his throat. "Please…please." He wiggled and shook his legs. It was his best attempt to free himself. One of the creatures spoke but in a language that he couldn't understand. The creature stood in front of him with his nose practically touching Langston's body. It grabbed Langston's face as he tried to look away.

"Ohwo erah uoyo? Ohwo *erah* uoyo?! Uoyo klawo no dercas dnuorg."

Another Desert Dweller approached. It had a shapely physique, as well as long braided hair. Hair that was beaded with one large feather hanging from it. Its chest and back were covered with body markings. These markings were grouped like short stories, combined to describe a larger tale.

The sand soldier walked with a commanding presence. Its stare instilled fear into Langston's being. It held a staff with tribal markings in its hand with a sharp spear on the end. The glare of the spear reflected on Langston's face. The creature walked at a slow pace; its subordinates formed two parallel lines. They bowed at the presence of their leader.

Langston swallowed deeply as he looked at the soldier. The sand soldier examined him before placing the tip of the spear on his Adam's apple. The blade pierced him enough to cause a small drop of blood to travel down his neck. Its presence filled every corner of his eyes. A thunderous roar pierced the ears of everyone present before the Desert Dweller could speak.

"Evaelo miho ebba! Evaelo miho ebba!"

The Desert Dwellers dropped him without hesitation. They lifted their spears and form a battle stance. Left leg forward and bent, right hand held their staffs over their left forearm. More Desert Dwellers appeared at the sound of battle formation: a thunderous stomp and alignment of feet and bodies. Back to back, chanting once more.

Langston fell to both knees and crawled to the closest cover. It was behind several bags of trash, piled high enough to hide him. He looked between the cracks; a mountain of waste. He stayed perfectly still at first, as he watched on - shocked by what he saw.

Peace within the Light

The man with the scar snored deeply, so much so that he woke himself. After scratching his groin, he reached to the side of his bed for ale. Yet, he noticed that it was missing and grew frustrated. He smacked his lips before he walked to the front of the station. He was oddly concerned about Langston's whereabouts.

"Told that boy sun-up," he grumbled, "shit."

Traveling in the Pines at night was not recommended. Most who wandered into the darkness never made it out in one piece. There was something about the dark that messed with your mind. Many things lurked; the seen and unseen. The man with the scar had seen it all.

There was only one direction Langston would go, and that was toward the walls of Hock City. So, the man in the scar followed in that direction. He walked along Highway 99 as if he owned it, with poise many didn't possess in the wilderness. He kneeled at the nearest sight of sand, and rested his shotgun on the ground. He grabbed a handful of the sand, rubbed it around in his palm with the tips of his fingers and then released it. He spoke softly as the smooth particles fell from the crevices of his hand: *May the flower of peace and light protect me.*

He walked swiftly, his pace fluid like the wind, as if he glided across the pavement. He felt that he was close to his destination; no more than a few yards from Langston's whereabouts. He sniffed the air. He closed his eyes and listened to the sounds of the environment to which he was immersed. A calming effect. Moments later, a loud but distant thrash rang throughout the Pines.

Pretty boy.

The wind rose beneath the man with the scar's feet. The force lifted him a few inches more from the ground. Maintaining his balance was a struggle at first. He knew at this moment that there was no time to waste, the Desert Dwellers were near. He pressed down, running with every inch of his muscle. The power in front of him was unyielding.

Suddenly, he saw what seemed to be Langston, in front of him; he was surrounded by sand soldiers. The sounds of his muffled screams alerted him. The man with the scar's eyes widened; his teeth clenched. He began to move again, but faster. Faster than the wind around him. Within seconds, time seemed to have stood still. He launched himself into the air. His roar was boisterous, even more ferocious than the largest predator imaginable.

Desert Dwellers clutched their weapons. They began to attentively look around, as they felt the thunderous vibration near them. They positioned themselves in battle formation, in order to prepare for what was coming.

The man with the scar screamed again, "Evaelo miho ebba! Evaelo miho ebba!"

Desert Dwellers wondered from where the sound was coming from. The man landed fiercely on top of some of the sand soldiers, crushing their limbs into particles. *Back from whence you came!* Arms, legs, skulls; fragments of what they were. But they stood again just as quick as they fell.

He shot slugs into the crowded area of sand soldiers, slowing them down but not exterminating them. Grabbing a sword of the fallen, he used it against the others. The clash of swords rang throughout the once quiet - and desert environment. Grunts and the octave of anger filled the air. The man with the scar thrusted and swung at his challengers with swift fluid motions.

Langston, in utter awe, remained hidden. With each swing by the man, Langston ducked. He moved his head as if he was in the battle himself. He lowered his head in pain after overexertion during one of his movements.

"Ouch, shit."

Suddenly, he felt a hand on his shoulder. The touch alarmed him; it caused him to raise his fist.

"It's me, Mr. Langston; it's me! C'mon, let's go!" said Jesse.

"What about...we can't leave him!"

"Hurry!"

Jesse ran towards one of the run-down homes nearby. The front door and windows were boarded up while the roof partially caved in. Movement could be seen from within, as residents watched the action from the darkness. Jesse pushed open the fickly wood gate, running into the backyard. In the rear was a car, behind it was a rusted swing and playground. The car, which was a convertible, and sat on its rims. Tires were stacked around the front and rear of it.

"Pull the top down! And the back seat forward!" Jesse shouted, as quietly as he could.

He and Langston pulled the top down. They then pushed the back seat toward the front of the car. A hole, carved out of the floor frame of the car was revealed at this moment. The hole was large in diameter - large enough to fit an average-sized person. Beyond the hole was even more darkness. It had an entrance that provided only a slight reflection of light, which led to a murky area.

Good grief, more darkness? Langston shook his head, overwhelmed with exasperation.

"Man, we really gotta go down there?"

Jesse tapped the edge of the metal frame with a rock.

Clank, clank, clank!

Desert Dwellers nearby heard the sound. Some rushed toward it. Jesse pounded the stone against the frame again, while Langston looked around nervously. He could still hear the war between the man with the scar and the sand soldiers behind him. A rope was thrown up seconds later – what seemed like hours later. Jesse tied the rope to the back of the car's seat.

The seat moved back into its original position after pulling on the rope. It acted an anchor as Jesse slid down, thus concealing his getaway to any followers. He dropped down quickly, as if he had escaped an event like this several times before. Any faster and he probably would have set the rope on fire, leaving Langston burnt to a crisp.

The thunderous noise of battle became muffled, leaving only a consistent vibration around them. The sound of water could be heard as Jesse hit the bottom of the tunnel.

"C'mon, Mr. Langston! Hurry!"

Langston pulled the seat back, grabbed the rope and dropped into the hole. He held onto the rope like it was the last one he would see. He swung from side-to-side while he hung, mentally and physically suspended in the air. He cringed as the Desert Dwellers ran past, hoping that he did not alert them to their location. The sounds of footsteps drifted from his ears.

Relief.

Darkness and Langston didn't get along. They were adversaries ever since his arrival into this city. He looked up toward the entrance, hoping to get a glimpse of light. A slight beam of light could be seen, but nothing that would illuminate his surroundings enough to calm him. He had to rely on his resolve; he slowed his breathing and kept moving.

Finally, his shoes touched a layer of fluid. The bottom was near. He let go of the rope and dropped a foot down into a few inches of water. Jesse continued to move ahead of him at a steady pace. He used a lighter to brighten the path ahead of them. The sound of rodents and other creatures of the night moved around them.

"Stay close, Mr. Langston; its real dark down here. There are lots of tunnels. You don't want to go down the wrong one!"

"What's down the wrong one? Jesse? Jesse?!"

Langston continued to follow, even though he was hesitant.

The sound of dripping water in the confines of a tunnel, felt like the whisper from a creature in the dark. It echoed on the walls and caused the hairs on Langston's arms to rise; torture. Langston couldn't help but check over his shoulder as he walked behind Jesse. He saw the same sinister, empty area. The more uneasy he became with the more he looked. He could feel the wind above him, as his fingertips grazed the rough interior lining of the metal walls. Soon the water that once covered his shoes dissipated.

"Over here, Mr. Langston."

Jesse walked up a set of wide steps, standing near a gate made of long rod-iron bars. At first glance, there was no way to open it. He banged on one of them.

Clank, clank, clank!

Langston gawked at Jesse's action. Scattered light flickered before them; in front of the gate. Some of the light darkened as a figured moved toward them. The figure became larger in size as it came closer. Its shadow walked parallel on the walls, as if the shadow was another person in itself. The figure held a staff with a bluish flame at the top of it.

An elderly, baritone voice rang out.

"Though light shines, it falls."

"Peace within the light shall protect us all," Jesse replied.

"You may enter."

The person, whom was covered in a long blue robe with a hood that hid all but its mouth - waved one hand over the iron gate. Its hands were long, dark and elderly. The gate opened, and Jesse entered without reluctance. Langston followed, but at a more cautious pace. He moved past the person in the robe, while finding himself staring to get a better glimpse of who and what it was. He peered into the hood, but could see nothing. Jesse yanked his sleeve at this moment.

"Mr. Langston, c'mon!"

The person in the robe watched as Jesse pulled Langston down the tunnel with haste, fumbling over the various debris around them. The person was gone when Langston looked back again.

"Who was that?" Langston asked.

"A Gatekeeper. We have to keep goin!'"

They arrived at another set of stairs after a couple of quick turns. The stairs shook and creaked with each step. At the top, seven doors were suspended in the air. They each were positioned around a circular platform.

Langston looked at the doors with much curiosity.

"What do these doors mean? Where do they lead to?"

"I don't know 'bout the rest, but this one goes to Hock City."

Langston looked at the door, and then back at Jesse with disbelief in his face.

"Trust me."

Jesse walked toward the door, pulling out a key from under his shirt that hung on a chain around his neck. He placed the key in the keyhole and then turned the knob. It was made of brass with a Trillium flower design in the middle. Specs of light released from the knob as it turned, in the shape of the flower. The door opened, but partially. Langston looked at the door then back at Jesse.

"Well, what you waitin' for? Let's go," Jesse said.

Langston scratched his head as he looked at the door again. *Welp, here goes nothing,* he thought as he pushed it open.

Hock City

Langston squinted his eyes. The bright lights of Hock City blinded him for an instant. The neon lights that were once miles away were now above his head. First he was bullied by the sun, and now he was irritated by artificial lighting. Once his vision focused, he looked up at one of the several illuminated signs. Some of the letters were missing.

elcom to Hock City.

The other letters blinked irregularly.

Many people were inside the walls, just as in the Pines. Men, women, children and more. Much, much more.

"So, these walls are they this high to keep the Desert Dwellers out?" Langston asked as he cast his gaze into the air. The walls reminded him of the stories about castles that he read as a kid. Dungeons and dragons?

Not this place, but close.

Jesse nodded his head in confirmation as he continued to weave between the people.

The walls appeared to touch the stars. They were made of a mixture of sandstone, concrete and debris. Anything that was solid enough to withstand the external forces, and that could be stacked. Around the top of the walls stood a lookout patrol. Members of this patrol stood near long hoses that ran from the ground. It connected to long pipes with makeshift funnels on the end.

"What are those?"

"Water. That's how they catch the water – in those long things."

"But I thought water was hard to get around here? Does it rain at all?"

"Yeah, it is hard. So hard that people kill for that stuff. Yeah it rains, but not often. When it does, that's how they get it. Those long tube things run down to the water plant. Water is probably the most expensive thing you can find in the city."

As Jesse explained, he and Langston walked down *777 Place* towards more establishments. The more the streets improved with the more they walked.

Langston looked around and bewilderment filled his face. The people in Hock City were quite different; their demeanor was unlike anything he had seen before. Hock

City seemed to have different residential requirements in comparison to the world outside its walls. Money was the main reason he assumed. *Stay outside of the walls peasants.*

Langston shook his face rapidly, in attempts to gain some composure. He felt like he needed to wake up, but he wasn't asleep. He overheard various conversations as he walked past.

"Get the fuck outta here if you don't have no lines! I warned ya' last time! Don't make me get my gun! I'm not playing this time!"

"C'mon man, I need those for the party lata'! I heard that Sadie Bell's is goin' be the place to be! I needs to look good, man!"

More conversations and outbursts filled the area.

"The sand people took my daughter! Please! Will someone help me find her?! Please, someone help me. I will give you all that I have. Please! Anyone!"

"I told you two to stop running through here! You are annoying my customers! Get! Get!"

Langston looked around and soaked up the scenery. The never-ending hustle and bustle. Insomniac surroundings. The lights of this place seem to always be on.

A fast-talking salesman grabbed his arm.

"*Hey*, how you kind sir! Come take a look at my goods. I got ale, I got shine, I got fizz that'll knock ya' on yo' behind! I got shoes, I got blankets, I got these crazy little trinkets... – hey nice watch! – I got... "

As the salesman spoke - at high speeds - Langston noticed people hunched over and leaning against the walls. Some were talking to themselves, immersed in full conversations. Others twitched while sleeping on unfolded cardboard boxes and blankets. Two odd-looking men fought over scraps thrown out in an alley.

"You got the last one! It's my turn!"

"You snooze, you don't eat!"

"I'm sick of yo' shit, man!"

The salesman had his merchandise displayed on the remains of a bus stop bench with a cloth that hung over it. For sale in his stash, was muggy water in soiled bottles, various canned goods, miscellaneous expired snacks and mason jars of ale. Random pieces of clothes: a man's polka-dot shirt, worn socks, penny loafers, a stained bra and more.

"I got the best ale in town! C'mon man, give it a go! You will like it, I guarantee! Oh, I know what you want – you want some action. Some *action* right? Hey, hey baby girl – come here! Huh, huh – how about this one? She will do you right! I will give you a discount too!"

Langston pulled his arm away, "No thanks."

"Hey, I know you need something! You *will* need something eventually! Everybody got an itch that needs scratching! You won't find better deals in this town! You got the lines, I got the time. Whether a rope or a gown, I can turn that frown..." the salesman continued his spiel as Langston pressed on behind Jesse. The further he walked away, the less he could hear of the sales pitch.

"What are lines?"

"What runs this place. What people here live and breathe for, outside of water. Lines can get you anything and everything. Just like water, they kill for lines too."

Jesse pushed up his sleeve as he replied. His forearm revealed a meter, represented by six bars. Six bars, made of six individual blocks. Each one resembled the equalizer on a stereo, embedded into his skin. All of his bars were full. Langston looked on in amazement. His eyebrows rose as he held Jesse's arm to get a closer look.

"Wouldn't money be easier? Money would be -" Langston stopped his statement unexpectedly, as he grabbed his side.

Jesse shrugged his shoulders. "Human money no good in these parts anymore. That's all I know. I heard about that money, but never seen it. We use lines now for everything," he grabbed Langston's arm, "You need water."

"Yeah, like yesterday. I need to sit down. I feel like I am hallucinating. That thing in your arm, these people – everything."

Langston could still fill the grip of the Desert Dwellers around his neck. Although his pain felt real, he had a hard time believing it actually happened. He had trouble swallowing.

"Madam Pearl gots plenty! C'mon. It's not far!" Jesse exclaimed.

Langston grabbed Jesse by the shoulder abruptly. "Are you sure I am welcome here? These people keep looking at me funny, like I don't belong."

"You will be okay, I promise - cause you with me."

The Line District

Hock City was once a well-kept place at first glance; but it was deteriorating due to the oddities and activities it contained. The cesspool outside the walls was beginning to seep inside at a rate that was hard to manage.

Despite the change, the city was adored. And the oddities? Some of the things weren't things at all. Some of the people weren't *people;* far from normal. Some residents stood two or three times the size of Langston. Some had more than four limbs, while others had more than two eyes. Some spoke with a weird tongue. Others didn't speak at all.

Jesse and Langston approached casinos and fancy establishments after traveling several blocks, and many roundabouts: The Line District. This district was behind a wide gate connected to an overpass. Above: patrols. On the ground: four guards on both sides of the gate. One way in and one way out.

The guards were equipped with various weapons such as swords and odd looking rifles. Rifles that seemed impossible to carry that were equipped with multiple scopes. The ground before the gate was a collection of dirt, but beyond the gate was stone. This was the only section preserved and you had to have lines to walk the rest of the way.

"Whoa!" said a large creature in a long trench coat. He had two vertical eyes, reptilian skin but with a human mouth and long jaw. He had a long scar down his face. On the sleeves of the man's trench coat were markings to show his rank. An emblem was imprinted to the left of the lapel. It was the same Trillium flower from the doorknob.

He held his hand out to the side to prevent Jesse and Langston from walking any further.

"Now kid, you know the rules. No wanderers can come this way. I shouldn't have to remind you of this," the man said with a deep, slithery voice. Saliva exited his mouth as he completed various syllables in his sentence.

"My friend is no wanderer. He works for Madam Pearl now – with me."

"If I don't recognize him, he is a wanderer. I don't know him. Besides, Pearl didn't inform us of a new recruit. All new employees come through us eventually."

"He is a Seeker, like me. Handpicked by her. You know Madam Pearl does what she wants. *C'mon*," Jesse patted the guard, speaking in his best persuasive voice, "I just showed him what we do outside the walls in the Pines. Just bringing him up to speed on things."

The guard stared down Langston with limited blinking - like a doctor examining a patient. He sucked his teeth in disbelief. He reached for his side, where a walkie-talkie was attached to a leather utility belt. He squeezed the button on the walkie-talkie causing it to chirp.

"Wait, wait!" Jesse exclaimed, "How about I give you some segments to let 'em through?"

"How many?" the guard asked with a smirk, as he walked back toward Jesse.

Langston watched closely, eager to hear more of Jesse's proposition.

"Um, hmm. Three segs. Yeah, three."

"Not good enough. A full line or I make the call."

"Okay, okay, a full line. One full line."

The guard looked around, and then slid up the sleeve of his trench coat. His olive skin was tough with large veins and scars. His lines were low with only two full before the transaction.

Jesse held up his arm, close to that of the guard's arm. He waved his hand over the guard's arm; a hologram appeared. One that had various buttons and meters. He pressed a circular button next to the lines. The word 'Transfer' lit up along with a brief beep. Suddenly, the guard had three full lines.

The reptilian hybrid let out a boisterous laugh, pleased with the transaction. "I gotta stop messin' with them girls at Pearl's. My lines low. I think I got a problem! Well, not anymore! No problem these news lines can't fix!" His counterparts laughed in unison, "Let 'em through!"

The patrol above the gate lifted two long poles. The poles were intertwined and designed to lock into the ground. The guards below were then able to pull the gate from both sides, creating an opening for the two to walk through.

Langston walked by the gate security apprehensively, sweating with each step. He didn't trust them or anyone else, regardless of the transaction that took place. Nothing about the people he had seen seemed trustworthy.

The patrol eyed him down as he passed.

"Lock it down!"

A thunderous boom swarmed the area. Dust particles rose from the ground and filled the air. The poles of the gate were dropped back into place. The sound caused many in the area to watch the activity. Who was the new person allowed through the gates?

"Man…"

Jesse frowned at his arm in disappointment. He shook his head while he spoke to himself. He worked hard to get his lines full. Endless days scavenging and errand-running. Back and forth, down roads and through various tunnels in Pineville. He endured much on his trips. Blood, sweat, heat and the smell of death that traveled within the wind.

"Those lines, how do you get them?" Langston asked.

It took a moment for Jesse to respond as he glanced at the ground between steps. He was consumed by his thoughts.

"My job is to find stuff for Madam Pearl. Anytime I bring something back she can use, she gives me segments based on what I bring her. Over time, each segment creates a line. Sometimes I help other people the same way, but they can't pay me as much as she can."

"How long did it take you to get those full?"

"Don't know. Long time I guess. I normally don't pay no attention. Been doing this since I was small. See that place right there...," he pointed, "...that's Sadie Bell's. People go there to drink and dance. Ms. Sadie sends me out to find anything to help decorate her place. She real fancy. Got stuff on her walls that I ain't never seen anywhere else. Stuff I haven't been able to find when I go out. Houlihan Dan - right there - he sends me out to find bones. He takes the bones and shaves them down real fine --"

"And uses them for what?"

"Dominos, plates, cups. Sticks people use to eat their noodles. He sells noodles too. What's up, Mr. Dan?!"

Jesse held his fist up over his head as he spoke. Houlihan Dan waved back quickly. He continued to pour noodles into small porcelain bowls. Customers stood in a short line, complaining as they grew impatient on the wait for noodles. The aroma was intoxicating; one of the only pleasant smells in the city.

Langston watched on inquisitively, "Well, why did you do that? Why did you give that guard all those lines? Especially since you needed them. Why are you helping me?"

Jesse looked around the district while he gathered his thoughts. "I had to, Mr. Langston. What else was I gon' do? Leave you there, knowing that you were alive and that you needed help? I like to help people. Besides, I can't have those guys calling Madam Pearl. She gets annoyed easily. It's better if I get you to her before someone tells on us. Maybe like everyone else, Madam Pearl could use you too. Maybe we can work together later."

"Dont know about that. I'm trying to get out of here."

"And go where?"

"Back to my home. My city."

"And where is that?"

Langston grew quiet. He didn't want to share too much, being that he still didn't fully trust Jesse - nor anyone else in the city. He changed the subject.

"This *Madam Pearl* lady runs this place?"

"No. Well, sorta."

"Sort of?"

"You have to talk to her. She can tell you better that I can. All I know is - she is impatient. And we need to keep moving."

Miles to Pearl

Rowdiness. The best word to describe the initial impression of The Line District. Lights flashed and beamed from every direction. The noise level was set to unruly. The ecstatic stench of greed covered the area like humidity after a thunderstorm. Lines, lines and more lines.

Lines formed to enter casinos. Lines gathered for boarding, food and erotic activities; the exchange of lines. Everyone needed more lines, but Langston only needed one - a line of communication. *Madam Pearl.*

He and Jesse came upon a large crowd. A spectacle gathered to get into one of the clubs on North Diamond Drive. Pushing and shoving – cursing. Objects thrown, fighting and more. All of this just to get into a venue; there were plenty from which to choose – any from short to tall – and from big to small. There was a venue for everything.

"Go around!"

"Wait your turn!"

"How many lines you got?!"

Langston studied the excitement. Jesse pushed through bystanders like he had done a million times before.

"A lot to take in, huh?" Jesse asked facetiously, "If you want to see some girls, Madam Pearl got a little of everything. If you are into something else, I can tell you where to go," he added with a smug smile. He nudged Langston with his elbow. Langston didn't respond. "This way, I know a cut-through!"

Jesse ran down an alleyway without notice, turned a corner and eventually opened a portion of a mangled fence. Someone had cut the wires to create an opening. It was large enough for him to pass, but a slight struggle for Langston.

"There it is."

Jesse pointed as he looked up at one of the tallest buildings in Hock City. It was a few stories taller than the walls. A skyscraper, considering. The building had a unique design: two adjoining semi-circles. In the center, 'Madam Pearl's' in big pink lettering. Underneath, in smaller print, 'Casino, Girls & More. XXX.' At the top, multiple levels of mirrored windows and black panels.

Langston examined the layout. Unenthused, he looked at another large crowd that was scattered between Madam Pearl's place and another venue nearby.

"You can't stand and look around like this, Mr. Langston. This is why people are looking at you funny. Try to blend in," Jesse explained, "We can go in through the side. I never go in through the front. People like me who work for Madam Pearl got our own entrance. We will never get in that way."

Jesse cut a corner and knocked on a steel door in a hurry, after bumping into someone passing. The sounds of commotion pierced through the entrance. Arguments and laughter, drunken behavior, slot machines and more. After another knock, a rectangular eye-hole was uncovered.

"Who the hell is it?" A raspy, throaty voice rang out from behind the door. Two beady-eyes and whiskers then appeared through the opening.

"Jesse!"

"Jesse who?"

"Open the damn door, Miles!"

The steel door opened slowly. It scraped the floor enough where the original color of the tile near it was faded. The sound of the door opening irritated Langston, like nails on a chalkboard. The sound brought everyone in the vicinity to a standstill.

Great, more unwanted attention.

Miles appeared from behind the door. He chuckled as he pulled the door wider.

"You play too much, Miles. I gots no time to mess with you right now. I gotta get upstairs."

"Yeah, you better hurry up," Miles agreed.

Miles held his belly as he laughed more; with each chuckle his large stomach shook. Langston looked on, stunned at Miles' presence.

"Somebody needs to fix this damn thing. This door is becoming annoying," Miles said, "What the fuck you looking at? Got something to say?" Miles asked Langston. He looked up revealing four long, sharp teeth - one in which was a gold replacement.

"Uh, um. I'm -" Langston was dumbfound.

"Langston, this pain in the ass is Miles," Jesse said before Langston could gather his thoughts.

"Yeah, yeah. Watch your mouth, kid," Miles said as he waved his claw and walked away. "I'm still your senior. Pearl's been asking for you. You better hurry up, ya' dig?"

Langston couldn't believe his eyes. The whiskers, the claws; he figured he was hallucinating - again. Just the lines in Jesse's arms was a shock enough, but now: *Walking, talking animals? The Desert Dwellers? The tunnel gate-keeper? The reptilian-looking guard? What in the hell was going on?*

Jesse could see the questions growing in his mind.

"Don't worry. Madam Pearl will explain everything. Trust me."

The two of them reached a hand-crank room with a lounge after walking down a busy hallway to an adjacent corridor - passing storage areas and other rooms. Miles stood in front of it, speaking to the elevator operator.

"Let 'em up, sweetness. They need to meet with Pearl before she blows a gasket."

The operator, a beige young woman whom was part-human and part Micrathene, slid open the doors to the elevator with both of her oversized, muscular arms. She wore a blazer with the sleeves removed paired with a mini-skirt. The blazer had the same Trillium flower design near the lapel. Fishnet stockings and knee-high boots. Half of her head was shaved; the other side was neck length and pink. Wide, rectangular sunglasses covered her eyes. She walked inside the elevator and stood next to the crank.

"C'mon. Let's get it," she said, with an impatient tone, snapping her fingers.

Jesse walked in casually, as he always did, while Langston stood still at the elevator entrance. He stuck his head inside the opening and looked around.

"Look, honey, I ain't got all day…," the operator told him, "You easy on the eyes but staring at your face won't get me lines. Either get in - or get left. Got it?"

Langston stepped in with caution. The force of his steps shook the elevator, even with his tip-toeing effort. He held the bars of the elevator walls with nervousness. The operator closed the doors with one swift motion, the same as when she opened it. She grabbed the crank and began to turn it clockwise; the elevator rose swiftly without warning. She spun it fast enough that it upset Langston's stomach.

"How far up are we going? This building doesn't seem this tall from outside. Do we need to go this fast?"

The operator stepped on a pedal beside the crank after a couple of minutes, in order to slow the elevator down.

"Madam Pearl's place; it's at the top. She likes to see and be seen. Her place is the tallest. She likes to know who is coming at all times."

"She already knows you're here," the woman chimed in.

The elevator let in a dim stream of light between the bodies of two guards, once level with the floor. They turned around, once alerted by the elevator's arrival. The Micrathene operator put the crank in the lock position and then opened the doors. Langston's face illuminated from the glow.

Pearl's Place.

Well, Hello Sugar

"Pardon, pardon me. Watch out. Move will ya!'"

Miles walked between the security personnel with confidence. His reputation was large, although small in size; he was cocky, but respected. He had the persona of a celebrity. It seemed that he said and did whatever he pleased.

He patted one of the guys on the arm as a greeting when he walked by. The guards, a pair of twins with large builds, stood firm. They looked human with the exception of long arms that hung beyond their knees. They had six fingers on each hand, light eye colors as well as multi-colored, earthy skin tones.

Jesse followed behind Miles with equivalent poise. Miles' presence made him feel protected. As for Langston, it took a moment for him to exit the elevator. The operator looked at him with a stare that reiterated what she had already spoke before the ride up. *Get moving*. Langston eventually obliged, but was halted after stepping onto the floor.

"Hold it," one guard said as the other blocked the walkway, "Scan him." The guards said and did everything in sequence. One turned toward a dark corner in the room; a woman lounged in a Victorian chair. He nodded at her. She then rose from her relaxed state and came toward them. She wore a vail over her face and a noir robe. She walked around Langston once. She walked twice. Langston looked over his shoulders as she moved slowly, in and out of his line of sight. She then peered at him with glowing eyes. After a moment of this, she sat back down as a signal that Langston was unarmed.

"He's clean," said the guard after receiving the response from the woman.

Two more guards stood near the entrance, across from the action. One knocked on the door with the back of his hand, while he maintained his focus on Langston and the others. He chewed a toothpick subtly, every so often spitting out fragments of wood.

Langston frowned in disgust at the gesture. He kept a close eye on everything that was happening. Miles walked away in another direction, speaking to various people he came upon. Jesse came to Langston's side with his eyebrows raised; a slight smile became a sign of sureness and relief.

The large, double-panel door opened from the inside. Lush curtains and flowers draped the molding around it. The smell of fruit and perfume exited the room, splashing against Langston's face. Jesse bolted in, like a boy home from school, anxious to get a snack.

"Jesse? Where you been, boy?" Madam Pearl spoke from a distance. Her voice carried down a narrow hallway into an open circular foyer where Langston remained. Multiple doors in the foyer led to other rooms. One room, with a door partially opened, consisted of multiple people that were in the midst of sexual acts. The sounds of moans and groans traveled into the hallway, along with the squeaks of aged furniture.

"I told you don't go outside them walls after dark, sugar; you too young. You can't protect yo'self from that riffraff out there, baby. I would be devastated if something happened to you. You understand?" Madam Pearl added with a southern drawl.

Jesse disappeared at the end of the hallway as Madam Pearl continued to speak. He responded softly, whereas Langston could only hear the subtleties of their voices. Minute change in octaves.

"Mmm hmm, mmm hmm, mmm'kay."

Langston put on his best statue performance, like the other sculptures in the room. His instincts told him that he should wait by the entrance. He figured he had to be welcomed any further, especially with security in the area; every eye on him.

"I see," Madam Pearl replied to the information Jesse provided her. "Well bring him in, sugar. No sense of keeping him a secret."

Jesse walked back to the foyer. "Mr. Langston, you can come back now."

Langston moved with caution down the hallway, past various sculptures, vases, paintings and floral arrangements. Lavish curtains, lamps, end tables and marble floors. Similar photos, like those in the man with the scar's station, were displayed on the walls. People hugging and holding hands, were glamorously dressed. Langston tried to get a closer look at one of the photos, but Madam Pearl could sense his uncertainty with each of his steps.

"Well, hello, sugar. C'mon back. You plan on standing out there where I can't see ya? I can smell you. I won't bite. I promise - unless you look like something worth sinking my teeth into." Her voice was heavy with added breath behind each sentence. She spoke as if she was just as large as her words.

Langston then entered Pearl's purple palace, or so it seemed, because of the hue of purple frequently used in the room. He was greeted by couches upon entering - one to his left, right and in front of him. These were positioned around a circular coffee table. A large painting of Madam Pearl was displayed on the wall, across from one couch, to which he cringed after seeing it.

Behind one couch were stairs that led to a platform. A bed was positioned, enclosed by long curtains. Large pillows covered one side of it.

Jesse stood at the bottom of the steps and waited. He held his hand up as a sign for Langston to wait, as Langston approached. Langston looked around more. He readied himself to meet the woman behind the voice.

He sat down on one of the wood-framed, lilac colored couches reluctantly. He admired how clean this living area was, compared to what he had seen during his journey.

Jesse ran up the stairs and pulled the curtains open on one side of the bed. A deep groan echoed in the space. Then Madam Pearl's chubby feet could be seen hanging off the edge of the bed.

"Help me with my slippers, sugar."

Jesse reached underneath Pearl's Cherrywood nightstand, grabbing a pair of fluffy slippers. He grunted as he struggled to put each one on her feet.

"Thank you, baby." Madam Pearl slid the rest of her body toward the edge of the bed. Her large, thick thighs, and massive ass were covered under a gown. She put her feet on the floor, like anchors on a boat. Not much control during the drop.

Langston's concentration was disrupted by the sound.

"Hold on, sugar. Let me make my face. Gotta look good at all times." The sound of a zipper could be heard, along with women's cosmetic products ruffling in a bag. "Okay, that's good. How do I look, sweetness?"

"Good as always, Madam," Jesse replied.

"That's right; you better know it," she replied, after giving him a kiss on the cheek.

She stood as her gown draped to the floor.

"Well what do we have here?" she said seductively. Langston did his best to hide how much he loathed what he saw. He looked at the round mound of meat, while walking down the steps. She was an obese woman, just as he thought she would be. She wasn't much taller than Jesse. Langston couldn't guess her weight, even if his life depended on it. She had multiple rolls of fat around her neck, arms and stomach. Her legs were large, solid like telephone poles covered in skin. Her face had full, large cheeks, in addition to an indent in her chin. Her makeup was designed was odd. Her lipstick traveled beyond the corners of her mouth onto her cheeks. Her eyebrows were unevenly drawn onto her face.

She came close to Langston and stood between his legs. Langston, uneasy, slid back more on the couch. She reached out and grabbed him by his cheeks; Langston jerked away.

"Relax. Let me look at ya.' Take that hood off," Pearl said, gripping Langston's cheeks tighter. She turned his face from one side to the other. "Oh wow. Get out of town. Are you. . .? Mmm. No, can't be. The texture of your skin. You just might be. I don't believe it. I heard somebody odd was walking around out there. You definitely were out in that there desert for a while. Look at those lips, dry as a bone. What lady wants those things on her? Jesse, go get me some clean water, cream and towels."

Jesse took off, running down another hallway. Pearl sat down next to Langston, stretching her legs across his. The heel of one of her feet grazed his crotch. She stared at him with inquisitive eyes, while she chewed on the tip of her fingernail sensually. He tried to move her leg from his lap, uncomfortable with her actions.

"Ah, ah, ah – this is Madam *Pearl's* place. You saw the name outside. I'm sure Jesse told you who I am. He better had. I can *do* whatever, *touch* whatever and *take* whatever I please inside these here walls," she said as she pressed down on Langston's manhood with the ball of her foot. "Mmm hmm, you human all right. Just different. Not like the others here. I think you gon' do just fine; working for me. Looks like you gots lots to offer." She gazed at Langston as if he was a prized turkey on Thanksgiving and ready for slaughter.

Langston jumped to his feet, causing Pearl's feet to fall to the floor. She let out a loud grunt in anguish, to which security rushed the room.

"Madam!" The guards shouted in unison.

"Work for you? What do you mean - work for you? I ain't working for nobody. Jesse brought me here because he thought you could help me," Langston said as he tried to back up toward the door. The guards blocked his path.

Pearl held her hand up as she gathered herself. "It's okay. It's okay. I got this. The human is new to the rules here." She reposition herself and relaxed on the couch, her legs curled under her.

Jesse ran back into the room at this moment, excited to see what had transpired while he was gone.

"Here you go, Madam! What…what's going on?" he asked, puzzled by the demeanor of Pearl's security, and Langston's body language. He put two bottles of clean water and two towels on the coffee table.

"Go get me some fruit, sugar."

"Aw man, I just came from that way."

"*Jesse.*"

"Yes, Madam."

Langston looked on while breathing heavier than he had been just seconds ago. He eyed the water. He needed it, but it came with a price. He then contemplated making a run for it, between the guards and down the hallway from where he came. He wouldn't make it without a tussle.

Jesse returned again with a large bowl filled with various fruits. Pearl grabbed a handful of grapes and ate several at once. She spoke to Langston again with the juice from the fruit dripping from her mouth onto her robe.

"You see, sir, to get some you must give some. You understand? What did you think - that you would come here, and then I would just *give* you what you wanted? That I would just *help you* for nothing, human?"

"Human?!" Jesse and the guards exclaimed, almost in unison.

"Yeah, your new friend here – is a human."

"I didn't ask Jesse to bring me here. I didn't ask Jesse for anything. He thought that you could help me. He said you were an important person here, like – like you're connected. He said you might have some answers."

Pearl let out an unruly laugh. She almost choked on the fruit she had been enjoying. "Important person, huh? Jesse, you told your friend - I was important?" She laughed again, "Well, important people don't become important by giving away stuff for free. Do for me, human, and I do for you. What can you do for me?"

Madam Pearl spread her legs and touched herself between her thighs. Langston frowned at her gesture. He took a step back, bumping into a guard. Madam Pearl became overwhelmed with laughter again.

"Calm down, sugar - I don't want your goods. It's fun messing with you, though. You not my type anyway. I like large men. Strong men who don't come to me for handouts. Men that bring *me* things. But maybe you can help me in other ways."

"Do for you? Help you? Look at me," Langston said as he did a one-eighty turn. "I have nothing to offer." Madam Pearl's security readied their weapons at Langston's sudden movements. "Jesse found me unconscious in the desert. I don't have any money, no *lines* as you call it - no nothing. Jesse, this is bullshit! I should have went back to that station and figured this out on my own. That man with the scar has been more help than this!"

Langston pointed his finger at Jesse and spoke with scorn in his voice. He spoke like a frustrated older brother to his younger sibling. Jesse bowed his head shamefully as he looked toward Pearl.

"Wait a minute, did you say...a man, with a scar?" she asked.

Langston realized that the next set of questions were vital, as well as his answers to them. His responses could either help or hurt him; the same for others. He calmed his anger and went into a strategic stance.

"Yes."

"Oh my. Jesse, you didn't tell me about this man with the scar - in the Pines."

"There is nothing to tell," Jesse fired back.

Madam Pearl raised an eyebrow, tilting her head in response to Jesse's tone.

"I'm sorry. I didn't think he was important. You talking 'bout that man in the station, Mr. Langston?"

"Yeah."

"I only heard his voice, Madam Pearl. One time. I swear. I only heard his voice. The one time I went into that station, someone grabbed me from behind and told me to never come in there again. They picked me up and everything and threw me out the front door. I walk right pass there now. I don't even look in that direction."

Madam Pearl walked over to a long window as Jesse spilled his guts. She looked out through the mirrored glass at Hock City and the Pines.

"So tell me, *Langston* – what did this man look like?" Pearl asked.

Reflect and regroup

The man with the scar exhaled heavy enough to make the hairs on his beard move. He looked around at piles of fallen Desert Dwellers, which were now lumps of sand. They faded as the wind blew. Arms, legs and heads dissolved into small grains. Grains that rejoined the earth. One Dweller would regenerate, as another one would fall. They just kept coming.

More sand soldiers were headed toward him. His instincts: fight till the death, but then he changed his mind. He no longer saw Langston. Langston was the main point of him being there, fighting endlessly. The best decision now: retreat back to the station and regroup.

He made his way back to the station as he defended himself from the remaining group of soldiers. He found solace in the rear once there, beyond the room in which he slept in. An office with a door that read 'manager' on the front. Inside there was an aged desk, filing cabinet, scattered papers and clothing. Common tools to repair cars.

He sat down at the desk chair and reclined. He drank a portion of ale from a jug, took a bite of a cabbage, and then opened one of the drawers to the desk. Pulling a picture from inside of the drawer, he dusted it off and then looked at it fondly. The straightness of his face, that seemed to be a permanent fixture, disappeared for a moment. He smiled from his core but did not let the smile rest completely.

The light from the room glared from the photo and shined into his eyes. The photo was of a man and three children, standing together in a grassy area. There were hills and mountains in the background. Smiles appeared on each face, with the exception of one person.

He cleared his throat and then put the photo away.

North of Hock

The man with the scar began to wake from his slumber. He had fallen asleep in the chair behind the desk; his legs extended across a crate. The jug of ale hung from his index finger. His breath was labored at times.

The sound of a wind chime woke him. A notification of daybreak. He rubbed his face, stretched and then rinsed his mouth with dingy water. He sighed as he looked at his coat, torn in some areas from his clash with the sand soldiers.

He gathered a few items and left the station again. This time he headed to a different part of the desert which was north of Hock City and the Pines. This journey would be longer than before. He had to make his way to a residential stretch of scattered homes.

It was evident, that some people desired privacy before the event, privacy of which they couldn't acquire living close to the racket of the city. This was a place where, at one time, only well-off people could afford to live. Large dwellings, now in shambles, were the exception of a few homes that had been maintained.

He entered the neighborhood and made his way beyond the row houses near the entrance. Behind acres of land were unique homes with abstract designs, all with long winding driveways. Most of the homes were in one piece, except for some that had debris in the yards, broken windows and missing roof shingles.

He arrived at his destination, a home with a sloped roof that had tinted windows and brown shutters. He pounded on the door with his hand, hard enough where the flower-designed Trillium knocker bounced on its own. Moments later, a man yelled from behind the large mahogany entrance.

"Dammit, Kinth. If you break another one of my doors, I will kill you myself! You won't have to worry about that riffraff in the desert!"

"How do you do that? How you know it's me, every time? That's amazing." Kinth responded before the door could open completely. "It has happened again."

The elderly man cursed under his breath and threw his hands up in frustration. He walked away from the foyer. He wore suit pants with suspenders, but no shirt and no shoes. He was balding with a hairy chest, along with a beard that hung the length of his torso. He wore small, round glasses while squinting most of the time.

"C'mon, c'mon. Close my door," the man said, visibly irritated.

"Another wanderer came by the station. The boy found him, but the wanderer came in on his own. It felt like he was drawn to the station, cause I know the boy told him that he shouldn't come in there; after what happened last time," Kinth continued.

"Yeah, yeah. Wanderer spawnderer. You and the stories you bring here. You are 'gon kill me before anything in this desert can. Always stressing me. Ever since you were little. I swear I am going to head further north. Maybe east to another corridor. Anywhere to get away from here," the elderly man said as he flipped through pages of a book. "One of these days you will have to visit that city again. You must face your past. The answers you need are there. I can only help you so much. My abilities grow weaker the older I get."

Kinth chuckled at some of the man's comments, but didn't respond to them. Rather, he gave a gesture of respect to his elder. He was accustomed to his random phrases and complaints. Instead, he stared out the door of the library while he listened.

The door led to a balcony that had a spectacular view of the surrounding land. In the distance, layers of mountainous sand covered by an orange and red sky. A field of cacti separated the sand from the grassy areas. The foliage moved harmoniously, as if it danced with the wind.

"What do you have for me?" the man asked.

Kinth removed his bag from his shoulder and dropped it on a stack of books near the man's desk. The elderly man had books stacked in every corner of his library. It was a challenge to move around without knocking them over.

"Potatoes and onions."

"More got-damn potatoes and onions. That sickening display of ale you make. When are you going to bring me something good? What about some cabbage? Where is the cabbage?"

"I ate the last head before I came. I will bring you some next time."

"Yeah, yeah, there is always a next time. I had my mind set on some damn cabbage. Why are you so greedy?" the old man complained. "What do you need now?"

"Something is going on. Another wanderer came by the station yesterday. These visits are happening more often. At first I didn't think much of it, but something heavy is happening. Whatever it is, it's not normal."

As Kinth spoke, the old man shuffled books and papers around on his desk. He found a notebook and skimmed through it leisurely, while he gnawed on a pencil. He licked his index finger at times, before turning each page.

"You must know something. You are the smartest man I have ever known, especially on this side of the city. Who are these people, and where are they coming from?" Kinth asked.

The old man leaned back in his tall wooden office chair. The cushions were faded and torn in multiple places. He picked up a pipe near the small desk lamp, and grabbed a leather pouch from the drawer beneath it. He removed tobacco from the pouch, sprinkling a portion of it into the pipe. He struck a match and slowly pulled from the mouthpiece. He spoke after he completed a couple of puffs.

"You have come to me many times with questions. Each time, you mentioned these wanderers."

"Yeah."

"And you have spoken to none of them? Why haven't you sought answers from the source? Why haven't you questioned them?"

"No. I haven't. I don't know. I spoke to the recent one. But the others – all of them – seemed lost. The last two walked by the station together. They were both trying to figure out where they were."

"Not all who wander are lost. Have you seen them since?"

"No."

"But you decided to help the most recent one?"

"Yeah."

The elderly man hummed to himself; he continued to peruse his book. Kinth watched him closely, as curiosity filled his eyes.

"I don't have a clue what's going on," the elderly man continued, "It appears that these people are not from the Pines, or that city. Obviously they are from a different corridor. Maybe they lost their way. Who knows? Maybe they were kicked out for criminal acts and reprogrammed. If they were headed to that city - it makes sense why you never saw the others again. That city - that city is a mess now. Ruthless. You know as well as I do that once they enter, their chances of survival there are slim. Their chances of getting out is slim. You know that, I don't know why you acting like this is new to you. I don't know how to explain what's happening. Why didn't you go with this new wanderer, and find out what the hell is going on for yourself?"

Kinth sucked his teeth. He frowned at the thought.

"But I thought that because of your abilities, you could sense things? I thought you could see events before they happened, or, see how things happened - when they happened?" Kinth responded.

"I must be near the energy of the event or the person. The life force. I can't do much from the confines of this home. Too much blockage. All the shit out there. I am growing weaker with my old age."

"But you chose to be out here."

"I know I did! I don't need you to remind me of my choices. I had to go - the same reason *you* had to go, remember? The energy in that city is evil. It's a mess."

"But I was forced out! You left before the madness became what it is now."

"That's what you say, but I believe you left on your own accord. And yes, I did choose to leave, 'cause I could feel what was coming! You don't need my abilities to know that some things are just not right."

"Why didn't you tell us what was coming?"

"Because the love you and your father had for that place blinded you!"

Quietness fell over the room.

"*Near,* the life force. So, you are saying, we can find out what is going on if I bring the problem to you?"

"Anything is possible. But you can't bring anyone here. No one knows that I am here besides you. It's safe here, and I enjoy my peace and quiet," The elderly man could sense Kinth's troubles with reentering Hock. "You have to go there one of these days; can't just sit and rot in that station. You don't want to end up like me – alone, forever."

Kinth scoffed, "You aren't alone. But how would I get in there? I can't just walk in."

"I know of a way."

Sugar Knows Things

"I *said*, what did he look like?" Madam Pearl asked again, showing her teeth like an animal that had been backed into a corner. The hair on her neck rose as she snapped her hefty fingers. At this moment, her guards grabbed Langston by his arms, holding him so that he couldn't move. Their hold was not as strong as the Desert Dwellers, but close.

Not again.

"Oh my, look at me acting un-lady like." Pearl spoke to herself. She waddled softly across the room with new poise and a straight face.

"Get off me! Lemme go! Tell your goons to get off me!" screamed Langston as he struggled to release himself.

"Please Madam, no! Please don't! He will tell you what you want!" shouted Jesse as he tugged on her arm.

"Oh will he now? Sho' don't seem like it. I will let him go, just as soon as he tells me about this man he met."

Langston pulled and moved more, but he had no luck on breaking free.

"You're wasting your time, sugar. Just tell me before I tell 'em to break you in two."

"Just tell her, Mr. Langston!"

The muscles in Langston's jaws pulsated. He looked at the floor to gather himself. He slowed his breathing and then glanced at Jesse with a disappointed disposition. He spoke after this moment, "There is not much to tell."

"Well, you better tell me somethin'!" Madam Pearl interjected.

Langston sighed before he spoke. He hesitated to reveal anything that he knew. "He was tall, dark, had a white beard and a scar down his face. He -"

The sound of a violent crash filled the room. Madam Pearl had been drinking during Langston's explanation and dropped the fragile glass to the floor. She covered her mouth with the tips of her fingers as her eyes grew teary at first. Then, quickly they grew bitter. She walked over to another guard.

"Let him go."

Langston was released, and shoved to the floor.

"This man, did he wear a coat like *this*?" she asked as she stood behind a guard. Her eyes were peaking from the side; one of her hands rested on the coat's lapel. She stroked the garment in an alluring fashion.

Langston gazed at Madam Pearl with a straight face. The eagerness that occupied her demeanor concerned him. The man with the scar provided aid to him. What was he about to offer him in return by telling her any details about him?

"I can't remember. I didn't pay much attention to what he was wearing." Langston stood up slowly.

"What about his arms? Did you notice any tattoos?"

"No."

Madam Pearl, waving her hands in visible disbelief, walked toward Langston. She chuckled before she gave him a sloppy, unwanted kiss on his lips. As she pulled away, a string of saliva came with her. Langston loathed her random act of power.

"You're cute, so I ain't gon' kill you. That would be too easy. Besides, I think you holdin' back information. So, with that in mind, you gon' show my men where this station is. You gon' bring this man back to me. And when you get back, we are gon' to have some fun. A big happy family," she said with an evil smile. "Put him in the maintenance closet for now. Gather a squad and take him to find this man tomorrow before dusk. If it is who I think it is, you will need a large group. Bring this man back unharmed. Take as many men as you need without leaving any gates unprotected. If this one is lying, leave him in a hole in Snake Valley," she added.

"Let's go, human."

Langston was escorted behind a set of double-doors.

No Windows at Night

It was business as usual in the Pines. Children enjoyed time outside in the sun. Peace filled the muggy air. They played hide-and-go-seek. Sometimes they played catch with dingy, plastic balls. They conversed amongst themselves about anything that came to their minds.

Nearby, parents and guardians of these children watched on while busying themselves in various tasks of bartering, gardening and cleaning. You had to have eyes in the back of your heads to keep your children and belongings safe in the Pines. At any moment, something or someone could snatch what you love.

"Did you see that last night?" a boy with glasses asked his friend whom was a girl with large, reddish hair.

"No, my mom doesn't let me go near any doors or windows at night," she responded, "She said there is bad stuff out there. Like - really bad stuff."

"My mom says that too. But I look anyway. I ain't scared. You missed it!"

"I missed what?"

"Those tall things came out again. I thought they were going to come and get people like before. This time they didn't. Well, they almost got somebody. Some guy. But another guy came out of nowhere and fought them! A tall guy, just like them! He had big, super-huge muscles!"

"Yeah, right! Stop lying," the girl responded in disbelief. She pushed him away, "Give me the ball."

"No, for real! He was hitting them, slamming them. Like boom!"

The boy began to make noises and movements to reenact what he saw. The battle between the man with the scar and the Desert Dwellers, which had occurred the night before. He closed his hands, jumped into the air and pretended to land his fists on the ground. He cracked the plastic ball as a result.

"See what you did?!"

"Shoot."

His mother interrupted him in the middle of his performance, plucking his ear.

"Ow! What was that for, Ma?"

"What did we say about gossip? Hmm? What did we say about nightfall and being anywhere near the door or windows?" Her questions pierced the soul of the boy like no other could as she became statuesque in front of him.

"Gossip drains the soul of truth. Truth is necessary for a happy life. The night in the Pines is unsafe, as where darkness feeds evil." The boy recited this effortlessly, but in a sarcastic tone, as if it was a school pledge before class begun.

"Good, son. Those stories of what you speak only make our lives harder here. If anyone heard about what you saw, they would take you from me - understand? We can't have that." The mother said as she walked back to her tasks, "No more talk like that. I mean it."

The boy, frustrated and embarrassed, smacked his lips in response to his mother's words. "Yes, Ma."

She kissed him on the forehead. "Love you," she replied before she walked away.

The boy wiped his face as soon as soon as his mother was far enough from where they were. He continued his story, but in a whisper so she could not hear what was said.

"It was awesome. I wish I could see that every night! I hope the man with the muscles comes again, and kills them all! So we can come outside and play longer!"

"You better stop. You heard what your mom said, didn't you? You gon' get in trouble again."

The boy shrugged his shoulders.

"I don't care. You betta not tell."

"Now we gotta find another ball."

Test Your Trust

"Tell me the way," Kinth insisted as he leaned forward to listen to the elderly man closely. He wiped his hands to shake off the crumbs from the stale peanuts he had been eating during their discussion.

The elderly man took another puff of his pipe. "There used to be a private entrance into the city, for government officials and dignitaries. You had to be one of the two to gain access. No exceptions – unless you were walking in with the man himself."

"I think I remember. A tunnel?"

"No, no. Above ground but hidden."

"Is it guarded?"

"I'm pretty sure it is."

"Well that won't work. You know I am no longer welcomed to that place."

"You will be, with this." The elderly man walked over to one of his book cases. He pushed one of the books on the shelves in slightly, to which a click sound followed. The book case divided in two, sliding in alternate directions. Behind the case was another room, filled with various expensive and exotic items. It was positioned on shelves along the wall. Plaques, trophies, medallions and more.

The elderly man grabbed a small black box from one of the shelves. "I normally don't reveal my belongings to anyone, but there are times when you must test your trust," the elderly man stated. He picked up a small black box and opened it. He blew his breath on the object and then rubbed it with a cloth. "There is only one thing that will get you in. You can use this, but after your journey you must return it to me."

He walked slowly over to Kinth with the box in hand. His old age was evident by the speed of each step. The polished state of the object reflected on the elderly man's face.

"This was given to me by the original Guardian. The true Guardian! Peace and light rest his soul. Its solid gold. It was a pleasure being one of his top advisors. Only members of his counsel wore this. This is the most valuable item I own. "

Kinth grabbed the box gently, and looked down at a gold, lapel pin. He read the wording on the pin, which rested around an emblem that represented Guardian's Grove.

Council Member.

The emblem design was that of a winding path, between trees and a ball of light, inside a Trillium flower.

"How am I supposed to return this to you, if I have to *give* this to someone - to get into the city?" Kinth asked.

"You don't have to give it to anyone! Use it, but don't forfeit it!"

"Why can't you just come with me?" inquired Kinth. "I will keep you safe; you know that," he continued.

The elderly man scoffed before taking a sip of ale, "Ugh. Disgusting. There is nothing for me there. And there is nothing there that I need. I serve no purpose to that place anymore. Now that his honor, the Guardian - is gone, and criminals have taken his place."

"I don't know why I am even considering this. One glance at me, it will be an all-out war. I'm tired of fighting.

Peace and light – we shouldn't have to die to gain these things. I am a wanted man there, you know this," Kinth explained.

"I know, but you underestimate yourself and what you can accomplish. Sometimes, we must go against the grain in order to gain the truth we seek."

Kinth scoffed, "Truth."

The Big Day

Click-clack-click-clack. The sounds of footsteps pierced through the door, along with lighting that shined through the seams. The same sounds that he heard coming into Pearl's place were present during his time held captive.

Langston rested on the floor, on his back, with his head tilted toward the sounds of muffled conversations and laughter. He did not scream out for help, nor searched for a way out. Instead, he lied there, and patiently waited for Madam Pearl's security to retrieve him. He had information she needed, so he was confident in his survival – for now.

He had been tucked away in a maintenance closet, joined by mixed company: brooms, mops, buckets, and cleaning supplies. Not to mention other items typically found in a hotel such as pens, pads and books of matches. Madam Pearl's logo engraved on all. He browsed his surroundings. The aroma of the room left his sense of smell numb for the duration.

"I'm on it!" someone yelled from behind the door.

Langston sat up and leaned against the wall, hearing the click of the door being unlocked. He watched as the knob turned. Then, the door drifted open. The odor of Madam Pearl's living area rushed the room.

"All right, let's go, human. Time to get to it," Langston was grabbed by the arm and pulled to his feet. He was pushed in the middle of three other guards - one in front, the other two behind.

Despite being held captive, he had a different air about him. His walk was filled with a bit more certainty than before.

The four of them walked down the hall, back into Madam Pearl's quarters. She heard the footsteps before she could see the bodies. She spoke to Langston before he entered the room.

"Well, good morning, sugar. Today's the big day. Are we ready to make Pearl happy? Because Pearl hasn't been too happy since you showed up. You got my people talking; asking a lot of questions. Too much unnecessary attention."

"No. Not quite."

"Not quite?! Whatever do you mean?!"

"The only way I help you is if you promise to help me get out of this shitty city. If you can't help me - point me to who can. This is the only plan I will agree to. Do we have a deal?" Langston held his hand out to shake on his proposition.

Pearl had been lounging on a chase, gazing out the window with her back facing Langston. A man had been scrubbing her feet, while another polished her nails. She spoke to Langston through a mirror on the wall, before getting up and walking over to him.

"Dammit! You buffoons got polish on my skin! Do I have to do everything in here?! Sometimes a woman's touch is the only thing necessary." She kicked one of the men as she walked towards Langston. "What makes you think I want to make any deals with you? I could kill you right now. Better yet, I could keep you here; make you my boy-toy. You would never leave my bed except to piss and fetch me what I need."

"Yep, you could have, but you didn't - and you won't. That man at that station is more important to you than your reasons to hold me here. He is *so* important, that you have kept me alive to find out more about him, which means you need me more than I need you. All I am asking is that once I help you, we part ways and pretend like I never came here. Whatever you do here, what your role is - I don't need to know. I honestly don't give a shit. All I know is, I am not a threat. I just want outta here. So, do we have a deal?"

Pearl stared into Langston's eyes, as if her poker bluff had been sniffed out. She smirked at Langston's play, because her hand had been exposed. Langston held a straight and she tried to get by with two pair, but the river left her high and dry.

"You think you smart, huh? Okay, smarty-pants; if you help my men get to where they need to go, I will point you to answers. I can't promise you they will be the answers you need, though. Most people think I got pull, but it stretches only but so far, especially with certain requests. In Pearl's house, what I say goes. Out there, in them streets and outside that wall – I have little to no control," she replied.

She lit a cigarette as she spoke. Then, she shook out the flame of the match. She grabbed Langston's hand, the two finalized an unfriendly agreement.

"I also need Jesse. He is the only person that can help navigate me back to that place."

"No, no." Pearl shook her head. "Jesse is not equipped to be out there for this. You on your own."

"Without him, I will be wandering for days. He knows where to go. He can cut down our travel time greatly."

Pearl sucked her teeth and then grew quiet. She thought for a moment before snapping her fingers. One of her guards left the room and returned. Jesse ran behind him.

"Yes, Madam?"

"Hey, sugar. I need you to go with your new friend. Help him find that station. Return to me right after you help him. Don't mess around out there. Do what you need to and come back. Understand?"

"Yes, Ma'am."

"If anything happens to him, I will string you up; gut you myself," Pearl threatened Langston, "Take them the back way. They already drew enough attention when they walked through them gates. Put that hood back on. Don't need nobody seeing what you really are."

Nothing Is Certain

"I think you should come along. You have a way with words that I don't. You can speak to these people," Kinth persisted, "I don't have the patience for that place. There has been enough pain and suffering. You know this just as well as I do."

"Oh, but you *do* have the patience! Why else would you be here, trying to persuade me? Hmm? You don't need me. You can handle this on your own. Trust me," responded the elderly man. "And trust the fact that I will kick your ass if you don't return that pin. And take some water. Can't drink that shit-for-ale your entire life. Your father enjoyed that stuff too. I'm surprised your liver hasn't given out already," he added. He shoved a gallon of water into Kinth's stomach as he pushed Kinth toward the doorway.

The elderly man enjoyed company, but only in short increments. He was accustom to much alone time, in order to think, to study and to write. To meditate and look into the energy of the life forces near him.

Kinth wanted to smile at the comments and gesture, but smiling was not something of which he was accustomed. For some time, his role in Hock City required a straight face. A face that drilled fear into anyone who crossed his path. By his logic, it would have been easier to escort the elderly man into the city while letting him do all the talking. He could have kept his head low, and provided the muscle if necessary; but his wish was not granted. His idea fell on deaf ears.

Survival wasn't one of Kinth's main concerns. He wasn't worried about coming out of Hock City alive. Facing his past was not an exciting idea; it wasn't at the top of his bucket list. He vowed to never return once he left the city. He had plans to move further away beyond the walls of that old gas station. Perhaps he could move to another corridor, but he was sidetracked by random visitors like Langston. Who these people were, and why they continued to walk by his station, woke his mind and his spirit. He had questions again, and the questions made him stay. He must seek the answers.

Hock City had the answers, supposedly, but it wasn't going to be easy finding them. He would have to traverse dark waters, while navigating the unfriendly type. Including his own demons. This could be a daunting task, but it had to be done.

"Don't worry about your pin, old man," responded Kinth, "I will –"

Before he could finish his statement, the elderly man slammed the door behind him and walked away. Kinth could hear the conversation that he conducted with himself as his footsteps grew quieter. He shook his head at the old man's demeanor. His demeanor hadn't changed much since he was kid.

"Good to see you too, uncle."

He made his way down the cobbled path, back toward the south sky. It wasn't tough to find the way back to Hock: bright lights underneath dark, textured skies. His fingers grazed the tall grass as he walked by the same homes that welcomed him on the way in.

North of Hock was peaceful in comparison to the Pines and the city. A place where kids once roamed freely on bikes and scooters, without worry of what lurked. Without worry of the grime that came with city-living. A place where on Saturdays, men mowed the lawn and on Sunday mornings, women hung laundry out to dry. Families ate dinner together, and waved to neighbors as they went by. The community raised the children together. Everyone trusted everyone or at least they tried.

A practice, and a peace that was no more.

He sat for a moment near the front gates of the estates to gather his composure for what was to come. Old friends, maybe. The unfriendly type, definitely. He took a swig of water and stared at the ground. The dirt was his canvas; it was where he drew out various scenarios. Sneak in, sneak out – unscathed. A battle was almost certain. What has changed in that place, and was he being overconfident, or not confident enough, in his abilities?

"Hey, friend, spare some of that water?"

Kinth's concentration was broken. He turned his head to the voice where nearby a man walked, pushing a rusty shopping cart full of various items. One of the wheels on the cart wobbled. He wore a long winter coat that hung to the ground, while speaking as he chewed on a twig.

"None to spare, but we can trade," replied Kinth.

"What you need? I ain't got much, and I like to keep what I got. Most of it at least. I'm headed to the heart of the Pines; plenty of things to find down there. Reckon I can find some water."

"Give me that hooded shirt you're wearing and your coat."

The man laughed, "You can't fit this! Maybe the coat, but what will I wear if I trade ya' this? Your coat doesn't have any sleeves! I would freeze at night's turn!"

"You got a hat in there?"

"Possibly."

"Okay, a hat and the coat. Here, you can keep the gun. I'm sure you will be able to trade the gun for a better coat before day's end," Kinth replied, as he flip the shotgun in his hand. He extends it to the man, handle first.

"Oh - no, mister. A gun for a hat and coat don't seem fair."

Kinth moved his arm again in a way to insist the man take the gun. Hesitant by the deal, the man grabbed the fine weapon. He admired the double-barreled shotgun which had intricate markings near the base of the barrels. He set the gun down gently in his cart, covered it with clothing, and then removed his coat.

"Okay, okay. Uh, I have this hat - and I got *this* hat." The man pulled out a women's cloche hat, and a kid's baseball cap. He shuffled around his other miscellaneous knick-knacks.

Kinth looked at the man with impatience.

"That's really all I got right now, mister, that I'm willin' to trade."

"What about that cloth right there?"

"This one?"

The cloth wasn't any old cloth. The Guardian's Grove design was embroidered in the middle. The same design that was on the pin the elderly man gave Kinth.

"I use that to clean stuff; you don't want that."

"Give it to me."

"Okay, suit ya'self!"

The man gave Kinth the cloth without reluctance. Kinth took the gallon of water, drenched the cloth, and then rang it out. He took another gulp of the water since he had the top off, closed it, and then tossed the jug to the man.

"I thought you didn't have none to spare?"

"I don't. The rest is yours."

"Are you sure?"

Kinth didn't respond.

"Well, thanks for the trade, mister! Nice doing business!"

As Kinth walked away, he put the trench coat on, flipping the collar up. He tied the cloth around his face so that only his eyes showed. The Guardian's Grove design displayed in the center, underneath the hooded shirt.

Period of Reflection

Back at the elderly man's home, he had reconvened lounging in his library. He spent a few moments puffing on his pipe, gazing at the horizon. He stroked his beard as he spoke to himself at times, reflecting on what was said between him and Kinth, as well as what he already knew before Kinth arrived.

He paced around his library, before going into one his bedrooms. He visited his closet to look for a box, which was hidden in the back of his wardrobe. He had a collection of suits, ties and shirts that he no longer wore. Vintage dress shoes, now components of a dust hotel. He saved his elaborate collection of clothes, even though he wore the same outfit every day.

He opened the tin box and gazed at the contents. Inside there were photos, trinkets and paper money. They were no longer of any value. A group of people stood in one of the photos, posing for the camera within a room at the Guardian's mansion for a party. There he stood, much younger, beside the Guardian and a woman.

The elderly man smiled at the photo, but then cursed at it thereafter.

"Brother, if only you could see the mess he made of what you built. All of your hard work, for not. Oh, how we miss you."

A period of reflection.

Wait For It

"Hey, where's the party at?" Miles asked in his usual cool, but upbeat tone. He stood by as he watched Jesse, Langston and Madam Pearl's men walk pass. He could sense the urgency by their focused expressions; wrinkled brows and tight lips.

"Shh! Madam Pearl wants me to go to the Pines," Jesse whispered.

Miles joined the group down the hallway. "With her security? For what? She never sends them outside of the city." The octave of his voice rose again, causing a guard to look in his direction.

"Shh. To bring someone back."

Miles scoffed, "Who the fuck is *that* important?"

"The man at that old gas station. The one I told you about. Remember?"

"Oh, right, right, right, right. That cat. But wait, I still don't get it. Why does she need him for?"

Jesse shrugged as he continued to walk, "I don't know. Maybe he owes her lines. Just about everybody borrows to play."

Miles chuckled to himself, "Pearl doesn't need lines from some random prick in the Pines. She has more than she can spend already. And with her connections to the Guardian - I mean c'mon."

"Just don't say nothin'. She wants to keep this quiet. You know how loud you can be sometimes."

"Yeah, yeah; okay. Whatever."

The guards continued to escort Langston and Jesse down the hallway to a penthouse elevator - Pearl's private transport which came equipped with carpet, a chaise and reading materials. The smell of body odor, machinery and perfume, clouded the wide space. It was built large enough to hold her and a few others.

"Neutralize and transport them," spoke a guard.

Another guard waved his hand in a circular motion in front of Langston and Jesse. Langston backed away from the gesture, holding his hand up to guard himself.

"Jesse, what the – " He and Jesse blacked out before Langston could finish his question. They were outside of the casino when they awoke. Langston looked around, puzzled at what took place. His heart rate was up, his body sweatier than before. He looked over at Jesse, who had a similar demeanor.

"What the f-?!" Langston mouthed to Jesse.

Jesse was just as surprised as he shrugged.

"Let's go to the armory, stock up and head out," a guard said to another.

"Move!" Langston was pushed in the back, "No more talking," the guard insisted.

The group journeyed to a section of Hock City that was quieter. It was more secure than the main entrance. The only people in sight were people in casual, uniformed clothing.

"What part of the city is this?" Langston asked.

"Looks like workers," Jesse replied.

"Shut up. I said no talking," a guard snapped back, "You two, wait here. Keep an eye, or three – on them. You two, with me," spoke the leader to his subordinates.

"You want to explain what just happened?" Langston asked.

Jesse shrugged again. "I don't know what happened. That was my first time doing that. Pretty cool," he replied. He sat down on the top of a backrest of a bench. "Man. Unreal. You are a human? Like - for real?"

Langston joined him, "Don't have time to talk about that right now. We have to get away from these guys," he whispered. He spoke while looking forward away from Jesse, while the guards were preoccupied with their endeavors. "Cause she is going to kill us regardless. Kill me, anyway."

"What are we supposed to do?" Jesse asked.

"We can't be in plain sight. We need to get underground. We have to get to the tunnels. "

"I never been back here before, Mr. Langston. I only know the area I brought you through. I don't know which way to go from here."

"How hard could it be to find a tunnel?"

"I don't know. I just know the tunnels I use. We have to go through the Gatekeeper's gate first. Any tunnel without a gate before it is dangerous."

"Dangerous how?"

"Dangerous because those tunnels lead to other places, like Snake Valley and Scorpion Lake. No one is welcomed to these places."

"So, these tunnels that lead to these other areas, are not connected to Hock City and Pineville tunnels at all?"

"I don't think so."

"Well we have to risk it. How much more dangerous can it be anyway? We can die here at the hand of your precious Pearl, or die trying to get freedom. I rather die trying to get outta here."

"I don't wanna die at all." Jesse looked at his feet thinking deeply about the situation. During the exchange, an old woman sat behind Langston and Jesse, on an adjacent bench, facing the opposite direction.

"Looks like you two in some trouble. I can help."

"Don't know what you talking 'bout," replied Langston, suspicious to who the lady was and why she offered to help.

"Suit yourself."

The lady stood and started to walk away. Jesse bit his lip as he gazed slightly over his shoulder. He looked at the guards who were still preoccupied, catcalling women as they walked by. He saw an opportunity, so he hopped the bench and followed the woman.

"Distract them."

"What? Where you going?" Langston tried to stop him, but was ignored. He chewed his finger as Jesse spoke to the lady. Jesse slid up his sleeve, and held his arm up reluctantly. The woman did the same.

"When are we leaving? Y'all not done yet? Man, those are some cool guns. Can I see?" Langston put on his best performance.

"Sit down."

Langston continued to distract the guards as best as he could. Jesse made a transaction with the strange woman. Thereafter, Jesse ran back to the bench and sat down, just as another guard walked over. The guard stared with suspicion at both he and Langston. The two returned to their original seated position - as if they hadn't been plotting an escape behind him.

"Stop moving. You're making me nervous," the guard ordered. He breathed his sour, heavy breath into Langston's face, "And don't get up again, human," he whispered.

"What did you just do?" asked Langston, "Did you pay that lady to do something?"

"I had to do what I had to do. That's basically what you just told me, right?"

"I hope this is good."

"Just be ready for the signal and follow me."

"But wait; what's the signal?"

Who Goes There?

Darkness crept into the sky while moisture filled the air. Clouds gathered in small groups. The wind gushed as it traveled through the greenery. Locals began to move indoors. The sounds of conversation and laughter began to fade.

If he did not hurry, what lived outside of the walls, would be just as much of a threat as what was within.

Kinth looked at the gold pin he was given. For a moment, it looked as if the design on the pin was alive. It was moving with his movements. He rubbed his eyes to gather himself. His uncle's words echoed in his mind, just as everything else that he knew thus far.

Since he had been living in the gas station, random people came by seeking help. Mostly men and women, all without knowledge of how they got there. Dehydrated, and hungry. Most of them, he didn't respond to or turned them away – providing no assistance. Many were never to be seen again. The others fell to the evils of the desert.

He approached the back entrance. It sat near mounds of sand, under tall grass. The entrance was connected to the same wall that enclosed the rest of Hock City; tall with random markings across it. Wanderers paced in front of the wall, some talking to themselves, shaking as if they had a nervous condition. Their faces were unseen.

"Hey! Hey! How do I get in here? Hey! You!" Kinth spoke to the wanderers, expecting a response. The wanderers didn't pay him any mind. They continued to pace back, and forth. "Hey, you! How do I get in?" Kinth asked again as he tried to get closer to the barrier.

"Step no further! You, sir! Stop there!" a voiced hollered.

Kinth looked around but couldn't see from where or whom the voice was coming from. At first he thought the voice was from one of the wanderers, but they were no longer in the area.

"Why do you approach?" the voice continued.

"I need access to the city," Kinth replied.

"But for what reason?" the voice asked.

"I'm not saying nothing else until I see who I'm speaking to," Kinth responded with assertion.

The force of the wind increased, causing trash and other debris to move along the ground, near his feet. He looked away, distracted by the sounds. When he refocused his attention, the wanderers that had previously disappeared stood before him. They had been perimeter patrols in disguise.

The voice spoke again, "I ask again - why do you approach?!"

The patrols took a forceful step closer to Kinth in formation. They held out their hands; spears formed in their palms.

Kinth stepped forward, unbothered by the act. "Listen I –"A guard jabs him in the chest with his rod before he could say more. The force of the jab knocked him to the ground. Kinth chuckled to himself, as he tried to get up, "Ok, ok. Look, I don't want to have to hurt y'all. I have business in the city." He was jabbed again.

"Ok, see - I tried to be nice."

"No one has business in this part of the city. Please go around to the main gate."

"I have special business. Why you think I came this way?"

The voice laughed, "Everyone in here believes their business is of importance. Go around before we have you removed."

The patrols performed an about-face, as they reconvened their performance as loiterers.

"I don't like threats, but I will let that one pass," Kinth dug in his pocket and removed the gold pin, "Is this *special* enough for you?" he replied as he held up the pin for the mysterious person behind the voice to see.

Security regrouped in front of Kinth in formation, after hearing a loud whistling sound. The barrier behind them started to separate, causing the ground to shake. Dust filled the air, darkening the area momentarily. Kinth coughed as he looked around, surprised at what was happening.

The group moved to the side upon the dust settling; a being appeared between them. The Praying Mantis. It walked toward Kinth, with an elongated back, and a partially human face. It had several antennas which hung to the side of its head, and it wore a long white jacket and a tie.

"Where did you get that pin?" the Mantis asked with a concerned tone as it walked toward Kinth. "And - my goodness, why do you have one of the Guardian's table cloths around your face?! Who are you?"

Kinth, slow to respond, put the pin back in his pocket.

"My business. None of your concern."

"Not quite, sir. See – any business you have here must come through me. Or, your journey ends now."

Kinth grumbled to himself while the Mantis looked him over.

"There is something familiar about this man. Let him in. If he tries anything, remove his head and retrieve the Guardian's items."

The patrol group moved to the side as the Mantis walked through the barrier. Kinth followed, surprised that he was granted access so easily. A blow to the chest was the smallest act of violence he had imagined.

"I'm looking for someone. I believe he –"

"I can let you in, but with that pin and that cloth, there is only one place you can visit. So, save your questions. We have our own, like how and why you have things that belong to the Guardian," the Mantis interrupted.

"Oh joy," Kinth replied.

The Mantis continued to walk, ignoring Kinth's cynicism. Mantodea soldiers joined the group, pushing Kinth to the front of the line. The group walked for miles, down a long, winding road. The road was paved in cobblestone with trees planted on both sides. Every so often they would have to stop, in order to fend off wild desert birds which flew over the walls at times to feed.

Kinth pulled the pin out of his pocket, and looked at it again. He held it up in front of him; he was amazed at how much of the design resembled the view in front of him. The design was an exact representation of the path by which he was traveling.

Though he walked inside the walls of Hock City, the area was much different than near The Line District. Cleaner air, greenery – peace.

Gotta Take a Chance

The sound of a scream sliced the air. The high octave penetrated the ears of Langston and Jesse. They remained nearby on the bench.

"Get off me! Get your hands off me!" a woman hollered. "Help, someone help!"

People in the area looked on, baffled, as the woman argued with a clueless bystander. She fussed, cursed and pointed her finger at a man while accusing him of stealing. She pulled and yanked away from the man, pretending he had a hold on her. A crowd started to form nearby.

"That's the signal!" said Jesse.

He spun around the back of the bench, pushed himself off and walked quickly in the other direction. Langston was glued to his seat; his thoughts had him consumed. He didn't know if he should follow Jesse, go in another direction, or do something else.

"C'mon, Mr. Langston. We gotta go!"

"This was your plan? We could have done better than this."

"Just c'mon!"

Guards made their way back outside after acquiring various weapons and survival gear. They returned with short and long arms, ropes and netting. They strapped on vests and other tactical wear.

One of the men noticed the disruption and immediately knew what was happening.

"Stop!" the guard shouted. He pointed in the direction of Jesse. His counterparts, who were previously preoccupied with the distraction, saw Jesse and Langston escaping. They began to run after them.

"This way, Mr. Langston!"

Jesse cut through small buildings, alleys and a market. He bumped into pedestrians and vendors. He knocked over trash cans, boxes; anything he could to slow them down. After several zig zags and turns, he stopped abruptly, seeing a large sign that read:

Water Collection

He pressed on with Langston close behind. Pearl's henchman were on their tails - shooting thermal energy bolts from HeatMods they gathered from the armory.

"Shit!" Langston shouted as a bolt flew pass his head. "What are those?!" The heat from the bolt fried a portion of the hair on his arm.

"HeatMods. They target body heat but don't work too well because of the desert atmosphere! Everything is hot! Just keep moving and don't run straight! Keep your head low! Hurry!" Jesse replied.

One of the guards stopped running, closed his eyes and clinched his fists. He reappeared a few feet away within seconds, directly in front of Jesse.

Jesse hollered as he was caught off guard but had enough time to slide through the guard's legs. The guard turned around in an attempt to grab him, forgetting that Langston was headed in the same direction. A collision followed after Langston used this moment to tackle the guard. He then struck him multiple times before regaining his footing. A tussle ensued before Langston was able to break away.

"Go!" Langston screamed to Jesse, pointing in the same direction in which they were running.

Jesse ran a few more yards and stopped again. He looked up at the large Water Collection building. Langston caught up with him, leaned forward and rested his hands on his thighs to catch his breath. He looked up and saw the building. Langston took point, running to the side of the dwelling.

"Where are you going, Mr. Langston?"

"See all those pipes on the side? They should lead to drains. Drains leads to tunnels. Whether the tunnels are safe or not, we gotta go. We gotta take a chance."

Both of them ran along the side of the building, following the pipes with their eyes. Most of the pipes ran through the walls and ended outside. At first, it didn't seem as if any ran into the ground near where they were. People inside the Water Collection building watched on at the events happening outside.

"Found one!" Jesse shouted, as he used his foot to kick the sand that rested on top of the steel drain cover. The sound of guards running towards them could be heard in the distance.

"How are we supposed to open it?" Jesse asked.

The sound of boots hitting the gravel grew closer. Langston looked around and nervously grabbed a stone that sat near the wall. He took the stone and slammed it on a rusty pipe, near a joint. *Bang, bang, bang.* Nothing. *Bang, bang, bang.* Success! He forced the pipe loose, but a gust of gas filled the air. He coughed, covering his mouth and nose with his shirt. "Okay, let me get the other end."

Langston twisted the opposite end of the pipe, releasing it fully.

"I'm going to pry open the drain cover with this pipe. When I get it open enough – push one of those stones right there under it to keep it open. Then, we have to work together to slide it all the way off."

"I'm not strong enough for that!"

"Yes you are; together we are."

"I don't know about this, Mr. Langston."

"You wanted me to trust you, right? Now trust me. Ready? On three."

Langston looked at Jesse, who in returned looked at him with squinty, concerned eyes. The gas was beginning to suffocate them and strain their vision. Langston motioned his fingers to count: one and then two.

On three, Langston used all his strength to push down on the rod pipe, forcing the drain cover up a few inches from the ground. Jesse immediately kicked a rock under it, but hard enough that it went into the drain. It fell into the darkness below.

"That's okay, get another one! Quick!"

The veins in Langston's arms and neck increased in size; he used the little strength he had left. Jesse ran and grabbed another stone. This time he used his hand, placing the stone between the drain cover and the ground. Langston's stamina gave out at the same moment as he let go of the pipe. Success again. They grabbed the drain cover, and counted to three once more. At three, the two were able to slide the cover free from the hole, enough for Jesse to get inside.

"Good, good! Go!" Langston shouted.

Jesse quickly climbed down the ladder inside the hole. At this moment, the guards turned the corner and were just a few yards away. They stood for a moment and breathed heavily – looking ahead to gauge what Langston was doing.

"I made it down!" Jesse shouted from below.

"Human, stop!"

Bystanders were alerted at the word 'human;' a word that many of them hadn't heard for a long period of time. They wanted to see who and where this person was. Unknowingly, they created a barrier by getting in front of the group of guards to watch the events unfolding.

Langston heard the guard, which prompted him to jump into the hole instead of using the ladder; unsure of how far down the tunnel went and what was below. All that mattered was Jesse was down there and safe.

The guards continued to fire rounds from the HeatMods. The shots, in combination with the gas, caused an explosion. It knocked them and others in the vicinity to the ground. The force of the blast shook the area, causing Langston to slam into the wall of the tunnel. This caused his arm to get tangled in the ladder.

Langston screamed in anguish, "I'm caught on something! Shit! I can't get loose! Just go – keep going!" He shouted to Jesse.

"No! No! C'mon! Free yourself! I'm not leaving you!" Jesse replied.

Langston grabbed the ladder with his free arm, pulling himself up enough so that he could straighten and release the other. He was then able to grab onto the ladder correctly, just as specks of flames and dirt fell past him.

"Just slide! Slide down!"

Langston widened his legs, so that his knees and feet hugged the outside of the ladder. He slid down rapidly as larger chunks of the earth fell through the hole. Commotion from the people above continued.

"Get him! Get him! What are you idiots waiting for?!"

Pearl Grip

Pearl's security forcefully made their way through the extravagant casino. They shoved gamblers to the side, without a care, in a hurry to get upstairs. They stormed into Pearl's penthouse without notice. There was news to share.

"Madam Pearl, we have an issue. We lost your Seeker, and the human," said a guard.

"Didn't I tell you fools to knock before you come in here? Now what happened?!"

"I don't know, Madam. I –"

Pearl shot him in the head before the guard could continue his explanation. The guard fell to his knees, with a gaping, bloody hole in his forehead. His eyes continued to move around. The last muscle reaction he would have. Others in the room scattered at the sound of the blast.

"*I don't know* is not what I want to hear! Oh my sweet Jesse, what are you doing? You, what happened?" she added, as she pointed to another guard, using a purple .45 magnum handgun, with a pearl grip.

The guard looked at his counterparts. He cautiously stepped back, creating space between him and the gun. He stammered before gaining composure, "Um, while we were at the armory, there was a commotion in the courtyard. During that commotion, the human and the Seeker ran off. We lost them after they entered a drain hole near the Water Collection area."

"Dammit, Jesse; them damn tunnels. I am going to ring his little neck. They are trying to get outside of the walls. That boy is really testing my patience. They are in for a real surprise going that way, though."

"Should we alert the Guardian, Madam?"

"No! No. We handle this *ourselves*. I don't need that asshole knowing about this. He already makes my life miserable."

"Do you want us to contact the Blattos? None of us can fit into these tunnels. It would be easier to work with the Blattos, since they are responsible for keeping watch on the external tunnels."

"Makes sense. Do it, but do it quietly. No more commotion, you hear me?!"

"Yes, Madam."

A Great Disruption

Back on the northern side of the city, Kinth was under travel restrictions from the Mantis. He was not far from his destination of which he did not plan on visiting: Guardian's Grove.

"We really don't need to go this way. This pin is not that important."

"Shut up."

A Mantodea soldier shoved him in the back to insist that he keep walking. Kinth was to keep quiet. The soldier struck him again when Kinth did not move as he was directed, but not hard enough to cause him harm.

"I suggest you tell your boys back there, to keep their funny looking arms and hands to themselves. Especially if he likes having 'em," he stated, after he wiped dust from his shoulder.

Offended by his statements, another solider attempted to grab Kinth, but Kinth latched on to its front leg at the same time. He bent it in a direction by which it was not designed to move. The injured Mantodea soldier let out an enormous wail in response to the pain. Other soldiers rushed the area, but the soldier at Kinth's mercy nodded his head for them to not approach. Any more pressure and his leg would have snapped.

"I do say, this behavior is quite unnecessary. Please, release the soldier," The Mantis spoke in a soft tone.

Kinth didn't budge. The soldier continued to squirm by his grasp.

"The pin that you have has not been worn by anyone for many years. Hasn't been seen for many years either. Very important people wore these pins. I'm sure the Guardian would like to know why you have it. So, again - please, release the soldier," responded the Mantis.

"Advisor, advisor!" someone shouted.

Kinth slowly freed the soldier; his attention was now directed upon the new voice. The Mantis turned in the direction of the excitement, while a Blattos soldier ran towards them.

"Yes, what is it?"

"We have received word that there is an incident in the city."

"There is always an incident in the city," the Mantis replied. He began to walk again in the direction of Guardian's Grove again.

"But advisor, this incident is of great importance."

The Mantis continued to walk, unconcerned.

"Advisor! There is a human on the loose. He and another has caused a great disruption!" the highly decorated Blatto shouted.

The Mantis stopped walking immediately. A look of intrigue covered its face. Kinth reacted in a similar fashion, but he was intrigued for a different reason.

Langston.

"A human you say? How do you know of this?" asked the Mantis.

"The Blattos army has been summoned to find the human and his accomplice. The two disappeared into the tunnels."

"Which tunnels?"

"The external tunnels outside the walls. The ones without gates."

"Insanity, no one dares enter those tunnels. Does anyone know who this human is?"

"No, Advisor. Madam Pearl's security had the human detained, but they escaped. For some reason he and another - entered those tunnels. We believe they wish to travel to another corridor, unseen. We do not know which direction they are going; my team is in route now to retrieve them."

The Mantis took some time to gather his thoughts. His antennae's moved in unison; the source of his knowledge and vision.

Kinth looked at the Blattos, attentively. He then looked at the Mantis, who appeared to be plotting the next course of action. Kinth contemplated the same.

"I should let them continue their journey, because they will end up making a wrong turn. But for some reason, I think we need to mitigate this situation as well. The Guardian will not be pleased. So, continue forward with this wanderer. I will go with the Blattos to handle this. Thereafter we will regroup."

Mantodea soldiers swarmed Kinth, grabbing him by his arms and legs. They pierced his flesh with their tibial spines, rendering him unmovable. Kinth could do nothing more than grumble in anguish due to the amount of pain entering his body. The power of the group of Mantodea soldier's grasp left him powerless, even with his strength.

At least he was closer to his goal: finding Langston.

Blattos

Langston and Jesse navigated the tunnels. They moved as fast as possible in the tight environment, unfamiliar with where the tunnels went and the occupants of each route. The only thoughts in Langston's mind were Snake Valley and Scorpion Lake - two places he didn't want to visit. The Gatekeeper, whom he encountered the first time he traversed the dark, moist tunnels.

The doors - the circle of doors, whereas Jesse had access to just one. The desert sand that he started out in nearly dehydrated and brought him near death. The people whom were now after him and Jesse; and now his attempted escape.

"I don't like this idea. These are the tunnels I told you were bad. Very bad. I knew a couple people who came this way, and they never made it out. If they did, they made it out -," said Jesse.

"Yeah I know – to a bad, dangerous place," Langston interjected, "I get it. I understand. But we have no choice. You understand? We have to keep moving. Apparently death can be at any corner in this city, so we can't worry about it."

"Hopefully we will pick the right corner."

They continued, with only a flicker of light provided by a small flame. The sound of small taps echoed on the tunnel lining. The sound was not close, based on its volume. Its octave increased rapidly with the slower Langston and Jesse walked.

"What is that?! What's that sound?" asked Langston.

"I don't know, but whoever – or whatever – it is, is coming for us!" Jesse replied.

The sound was that of Blattos soldiers, gaining ground on their location. The two ran faster, taking larger strides in the almost knee-high water. The flame, at times, would disappear due to the force of the wind that was increased by the running, as well as the moisture that swept the tunnels.

"Man, man, man, man – I don't know which way to go," Jesse spoke nervously. He looked around, flicking the lighter again. "Which way you think?"

"Gimme." Langston snatched the lighter from Jesse and took the lead.

The Blattos grew closer. The sound they made was as if hundreds of people were typing on a typewriter at once. A sound that was intense and unnerving in the darkness.

"I got an idea!" Jesse exclaimed, "Let me see it," he added as he reached his hand out to take the lighter back.

"What you doing?! We can't see!"

"Hold on," Jesse replied as he closed the cap of the lighter. Then he banged it on the tunnel wall. A loud hissing sound started to make its way to them after a moment of unnerving silence. Langston banged on the walls again and the sound grew louder.

"What are you doing?!"

"If this is a dead end, it won't just be for us."

The two of them ran toward the sound, assuming that it would lead to an exit - regardless of what waited by the exit. Suddenly, the earth began to shake around them. Muffled voices could be heard, just before the light they were following started to disperse. The sound of Blattos was now in front of them, just as in the rear.

A deep rumble occurred, and then a large piece of the tunnel was smashed into them. Dirt, gravel and various debris fell on Langston and Jesse, right before they were swarmed by the Blattos. Langston fought off as many as he could, but the Blattos were able to increase and decrease their size as needed; a defense mechanism they used when in battle.

The Mantis approached from above once Langston and Jesse were held captive. Mantodea soldiers and Madam Pearl's security stood nearby. The hissing sound was not from an exit point, but rather from the Mantis.

"Well. So...it *is* true. A human. I can't believe it. Never thought I would see one of you with my own eyes. It's been many, many years."

The Mantis made the hissing sound again, which sent a chill to run through Langston's body. The Mantis then spread its wings as the hissing amplified. It was an intimidation tactic that seemed to work without much effort. Langston and Jesse prepared for the worse.

"Pull them out quickly, before we have other, unnecessary company. Put them with the other, and then refill the hole. Tie these two up and keep them separated -

put them in line with the other. We will take all three of them to see the Guardian. Tell Pearl to meet us there. We have questions for her that she needs to answer."

Langston and Jesse were bound by the wrists and feet, and placed between the groups of soldiers.

The Paved Road

Kinth rested on the ground against a wall. He was near a winding, paved road with large red stones. The road to Guardian's Grove. He relaxed, with his head against the dwelling, as he admired the landscape and nature. He felt peace for a moment. The peace reminded him of when he was young, when Hock City wasn't infested with greed and madness.

He thought about his decision to come back to the city. Was it worth it? The struggle, that was almost certain? He shuffled rocks and pebbles in his hand while In the midst of his thoughts, impatient with sitting stagnant. He waited and wondered about what would occur next. His displeasure grew uncontrollable.

"Why we still sittin' here? Can we get movin?' Just kill me or let me go."

The Mantodea soldiers had taken another break from the travel; Kinth did not know the reason. They ignored his comments, as they spoke amongst themselves, scanning the area for any threats. Kinth repeated himself, and started to purposely provoke the soldiers.

"Hey! I'm talking to you insect-boy! You know that if it was just us - one-on-one, I could take you, right? Ya' know that right? You girly - ugly looking things."

He threw a stone at the head of the soldier, but missed his target. He tried again, but the stone only grazed it. The graze was enough for the soldier to turn around annoyed and face him. It spread its wings and hissed at his actions.

Other soldiers followed suit once they were alerted. Their actions didn't daunt Kinth. He dropped the rest of the rocks, and wiped his hands together as he stood.

"Oh, you didn't like that, huh?! What you gon' do about it? Huh? Let's go!" said Kinth as he instigated the situation. He put one leg back in a fighting stance and balled his fists.

"Enough!" a voice shouted.

The soldiers folded their wings, and bowed their heads, as they turned their attention to the voice. Kinth, looked on with a smug smile. The voice was that of the Mantis, returning with Langston and Jesse. At first, Kinth didn't notice Langston because of the tussle that was seconds away from occurring.

The Mantis approached Kinth slowly. He leaned in, just inches away from Kinth's face, speaking in a villainous tone.

"I have two others that will be joining you."

Kinth observed the view over the Mantis' shoulder. He noticed Langston and Jesse, walking sluggishly between several Mantodea soldiers. He did not change the smug expression on his face, despite this revelation. Rather, he wanted to avoid exposing the truth that he knew them. He sucked his teeth as if he didn't care, despite the frustration that lied beneath his poised demeanor.

The same couldn't be said of Langston. As soon as he noticed Kinth, he spoke his name not out loud but to himself. He spoke it loud enough for a soldier to hear him, to which this soldier alerted the others of what was said.

"Advisor, it seems the human knows the other captive."

"Doesn't matter; each of them will be dealt with by the Guardian," responded The Mantis, unbothered.

The soldiers regrouped behind The Mantis on the paved road, between the trees. Due to his ferociousness and uncooperative nature, Kinth was bound between soldiers at the front of the line. Langston and Jesse were behind them.

"Sir, how do you suppose these three came into contact? How do you think the human got here?" asked a soldier.

"I don't like to speculate, soldier. These matters will be discussed in the proper forum. Back to your position," replied The Mantis.

"Yes, Advisor."

The road started to widen; the trees became taller. The group approached a roundabout. Tall brick pillars with statues were positioned on both sides. The statues were abstract in design. A wide, iron-gate with the Guardian's crest centered on the front was protected by multiple guards. Behind the gate, the Guardian's mansion; a unique three-story Victorian structure, tan with several windows. The mansion sat at the top of a hill. It had wide steps that led to the doorway.

Jesse was surrounded by what seem to be the tallest soldiers in the group. He did his best to look around them to see the mansion. He had heard about this place, but hadn't seen it with his own eyes. He relied solely on his imagination to envision what this area looked like.

Pearl had spoken of the Guardian plenty of times, but he had never seen the face of the mysterious man. Because of these reasons, his excitement got the best of him - causing him to run toward the gate.

"Hey! Somebody get him! Good grief!" yelled one of the Mantodea soldiers.

Jesse hopped from the line, dodging the soldier's grasps by moving underneath their legs. A soldier yanked on the chain to which he was tied, causing him to fall to the ground just short of the entrance. He looked up at the mansion while he lied there, on his back.

"Enough of this! Move out of line again, and you won't need to see the Guardian. I will deal with you myself. Open the gate!" spoke The Mantis in an aggravated state.

The opening of the gate rang loud, like the cry of an injured bird. Both Kinth and Langston watched on, as Jesse was lifted into the air. He was carried the rest of the way, like a pig headed to roast, to avoid further disturbances.

"Let's go!" shouted a soldier.

The group marched in formation through the gates, and around both sides of the roundabout. The soldiers were put at ease after an about face.

"You six - with me. The rest of you position yourselves around the courtyard - and please - no more surprises," The Mantis said.

The Mantis, soldiers and captives traveled up the steps, toward the front of the mansion. As they approached the entrance - the wide double-doors, with decorative stained glass, opened automatically once they were a few feet from them. Inside, two women with butterfly wings, stood on each side of the door. They neither greeted the Mantis, nor did they make any sound.

The foyer was designed as a roundabout, just like in the courtyard. A large, well-polished wood table was centric to the room, with a bust of a man positioned in the middle; a floral arrangement centered around it. A chandelier hung above, in addition to large globes that contained candles inside each one.

The man was middle-aged, based on the appearance of the bust. He had a narrow face, long nose and a strong jaw. He had an annoyed expression, as if he was not pleased with posing for the sculpture. He was disgusted with something while the bust was being created. He had wavy hair, prominent wrinkles in his forehead and no facial hair except for a thin mustache and eyebrows.

"Sit there," a solider instructed, pointing to a bench in the room. Kinth sat, while Langston and Jesse were put in a separate area. They were placed on the adjacent side of the mansion. The two of them sat nervously beside one another. Jesse tapped his feet, while Langston scanned the fixtures and the intricate style of the room.

"It seems this is where most of the money is going in this city," Langston stated. He lounged against the foyer wall. "A damn shame. To live like this, with all those people out there in need."

"Well, sugar, I knew one of these days you would get yourself into trouble — trouble that momma may not be able to get you out of," Pearl's voice traveled around the corner before she was seen, between the sound of slurps as she enjoyed a drink. "Mmm, mmm, mmm. Boy, what am I gon' do wit' you?"

Jesse flinched as he felt her hand stroke his head. He had no idea what to expect next. He knew he was no longer Pearl's beloved helper. Pearl gradually revealed herself holding a martini glass. She stared at Jesse as she drank more, and then positioned herself between his legs.

"I told you don't ever lie to me, didn't I, sugar? And to always, *always* follow my instructions." She forcefully squeezed his cheeks, to remind him of the kid that he was. His lips bulged as they stuck out like a sea creature.

"Please, Madam Pearl —" Jesse tried to speak but couldn't get out much.

"Leave the kid alone; I told him to do what he did. Why don't you come and grab me like that? See what happens," Langston rested his head against the wall, looking out the corner of his eye while speaking with more confidence than when they first met.

"Shut up! I wasn't talking to you. You goddamn trouble-maker. If I had my gun - We will deal with you sh–"

"Pearl, please…," a new, calm voice entered the space. The voice was smooth, quiet and mild in tone. "Let's not taunt our guests."

Pearl removed her grasp from Jesse's face as she stepped away. She cut her eyes at him and Langston, just as a new set of guards, in three-piece suits, entered the space. Once in their position, the sound of another set of footsteps grew closer. A man approached Pearl slowly with his back turned toward everyone else. He whispered something in her ear, and in response, she walked away.

He turned around and faced Langston and Jesse, staring at them for several seconds before saying anything. He looked into a mirror and patted an out-of-place portion of his hair. He pulled on the sleeves of his shirt to adjust the length, ensuring that they extended enough beyond the sleeves of his suit jacket. He straightened the Windsor knot of his tie.

"There, that's better. I clean up well, if I do say so myself. Oh, my apologies. Hi. I'm the Guardian. Pleased to meet you."

It Is Me

"Um, hello - sir," replied Jesse. He was excited but cautious in the same breath. He finally met the man face-to-face that he had heard about. The Guardian. The Legend. The man that most people in Hock City feared. His reputation preceded him.

The Guardian reached his hand out towards him and they shook hands.

"Nice grip, young man," the Guardian said as he wiped his hand clean from the moisture of Jesse's hand.

"No need to be uneasy. Everyone is safe and welcome in the Guardian's mansion. Without the people, we are nothing, because the people always provide something."

He reached out to Langston next, but Langston did not oblige as easy as Jesse. He remained quiet and unimpressed.

"You, sir - you must be...*Langston*, is it?" he asked. He pointed his index finger in Langston's direction.

Langston sat with his arms folded and his legs crossed, stretched out in front of him. He turned his gaze to the Guardian, but then looked away.

"My name is unimportant."

"Au contraire, my friend. Everyone's name is important, for different and various reasons. We are new friends, right? And friends know each other's name, and greet each other accordingly, correct? So," the Guardian cleared his throat, "...with that said - shake my hand."

Langston looked at the Guardian's hand, then back at his face. The two of them locked eyes, for a short game of 'who had the most power.' A stare down contest of sorts.

"Tell you what - you shake my hand and I won't kill you; how is that? Besides, I don't want to stain that exquisite marble wall behind you. It took my men a long, long time - to gather the stones needed to make that. You know how priceless some things can be."

"Why does everyone in this city threaten or expect violence? What is wrong with you people? I haven't hurt anyone."

The Guardian didn't respond. Instead, he kept his hand extended, waiting for Langston to acknowledge and meet his order. Langston shook the Guardian's hand, aware that he wasn't making any strides with his argument.

The Guardian won this round.

"Excellent. I'm glad you agree. We have to work together, because together - we are better," the Guardian clapped his hands once, "Mantis, I was told that we have another guest? Yes? Where is he?"

"To avoid any further troubles, we separated him from these two. He is in your reception room, Guardian."

"Troubles, you say?"

"Yes, but nothing you need to concern yourself with, sir."

The Guardian studied the Mantis for a moment, as if the Mantis had more to say. As if the troubles of which he spoke were more than just troubles. After this pinch of silence, the Guardian walked toward another set of doubled-doors. These doors led to the reception room of the mansion where Kinth waited.

The winged-women opened both doors; they bowed their heads to the Guardian's presence.

"Well, now, who is our other friend?"

Mantodea soldiers, along with the guards in three-piece suits, stood watch around the room. They enclosed Kinth in a semi-circle, with every eye monitoring his behavior. He was treated as if he was the biggest threat to all of Hock City and Pineville. A bomb that was on the brink of detonating.

Kinth looked at pictures on the wall, and spoke with his back turned. "How have you been, *brother*?"

"Kinth?" The Guardian's knees weakened, as Kinth's voice resonated. He slid down the arm of a chair, and sat as beads of sweat started to form on his brow.

"Yes, brother. It is me."

"Pearl!" The Guardian's voice cracked, as he shouted toward the double-doors, "Go get Pearl; now!" Guards marched toward the doors, but stopped suddenly.

"I'm right here, you prick." Pearl strolled toward the room leisurely, sipping on a second martini. "I needed to top off my drink. What is it? Can me and Jesse go yet?"

Kinth stood like a statue in the center of the room, with his arms crossed behind his back. Pearl noticed him after taking a sip of her drink. Then, her feet became like concrete.

"Oh sweet biscuits; I knew it."

"Pearl," said Kinth, "I see you haven't changed since the last time I saw you, sister."

Pearl walked towards Kinth slowly with one hand over her mouth and a martini glass in the other. She was stunned by his presence. Tears began to fill her eyes, as she got a closer look at his face. Hesitantly, she reached out to touch him. He pushed her hand away, frightening her, as her fingers grazed his sleeve. She yelped as she smacked him, and then forced a hug.

Security was alerted after The Guardian snapped his fingers.

"How could you leave us?!" Pearl asked, with her head on Kinth's chest. Kinth stepped back, breaking the embrace.

"Leave *you*, leave *you*?" he scoffed, "I did not leave you. The actions involving our father forced me out."

"What is he talking about?" Pearl asked the Guardian. "You told me Kinth left on his own accord."

"Kinth, please brother," The Guardian spoke with distress. "Let's talk this out."

"There is nothing for us to talk about, *brother* - other than what you did. What you did to this family. And what I am owed."

"We can fix this," The Guardian replied.

"No. What you did can't be fixed. No more talk."

"What is going on? I don't understand. Please, somebody, tell me what's happening," said Pearl.

The Guardian looked at Pearl, and then back at Kinth. Kinth balled his fist, annoyed more with each second in the Guardian's presence. His body filled with rage.

"Oh, you don't, Pearl?" Kinth turned toward the Guardian, stunned, "Really, brother? You kept your own sister out of the loop? Your own flesh and blood. Does she even know about dad? What did he tell you Pearl, hmm? That dad died of old age, or something else? That he is out on another journey? Exploring? One of those journeys that kept him gone for many cycles at a time?" Kinth spoke to Pearl with scorn in his eyes. Then he looked back at the Guardian, "You killed our father! All so you can sit where he sat at the head of the table. I was the next in line to reign, and you robbed me of that! You robbed this city of the good it had! I want what's rightfully mine. My father's seat! You have a lot of explaining to do!"

The Guardian scoffed, "*Rightfully yours*. Ha! Explain what? I don't have to explain shit."

"Oh, brother, you will – you will explain. Eventually. There are many questions I have for you. Like, the human in the foyer. Who is he?"

"I care nothing for the circumstances involving him or that boy." The Guardian snapped his fingers again. This time, the guards moved in closer to Kinth and put their weapons within an inch of his body.

"Like old times, huh, brother? What a great reunion this is. You haven't changed. You have been violent all your life. Here we stand as men, amongst the same issues we had as kids. You destroy everything you touch." Kinth spoke freely as guards stood nervously, unsure of what Kinth may do. They practically shook at his aggressiveness with each of his movements.

"Please, no! No, Franklin! No more of this! We are family for Pete's sake! Embrace your brother! He came home! We can start over! We can fix the bond that was broken!" Pearl exclaimed. She showed a vulnerable side that many had not seen at all; and, for others, not in some time.

"It's 'Guardian' to you! You fat waste of space! You will address me as such!"

"Ha, Guardian! You are no Guardian; you are nothing but a liar and a murderer!" Kinth snapped back.

"Call me what you will. It doesn't matter. I run this city now. So why should I listen to you? Hmm? Why should I listen to him, Pearl? Why should I have any discussion with your precious brother?"

"I was given the leftovers to everything when dad was alive. I was always thought of last; treated like last place. Like, like - like an outcast. You and Pearl were his favorites. Couldn't do anything without advice from Kinth, and Pearl – you could practically do whatever you wanted!

The only girl. Spoiled. *Fa, la, la, la, la.* That's all you did - was walk around singing because you got what you wanted. But me, oh – no! I was ordered around like a slave! Do this, go there and get me that! Gimme a break of this pathetic, emotionally-driven, entitlement bullshit." The Guardian spoke with spite; his eyes turned as red as a fiery sky.

"You can't fault me for dad's actions! I tried to be a good brother, but you didn't see me as such! You saw me as your enemy, or your competition - just like everyone else that you were jealous of! I stood up for you plenty of times. I cleaned up the messes you made. I took the blame for a lot of your shit! Do you remember nothing but what benefits you?" Kinth contested.

"Sure you did. Enough of this! I'm done with this!" The Guardian stood from the chair, regaining his authority. The guards nearby pointed their weapons at Kinth. "I don't have to explain anything. I don't owe you *anything*. You've been gone too long, brother. Take him away to the cellar for now! I will figure out what to do with him later. And bring the other two in here. Wait, no – just bring the human. Put the boy in the cellar too. I don't need to speak to him. At least not yet."

"Please no! Not Jesse! Don't hurt my Jesse!"

"Shut up, Pearl. You know what - take her too. Tired of looking at your face. Lock her in the guest room and keep her there. Send a few of our guys to secure her casino. Lock up her lines. Kill anyone that gets in your way," The Guardian snapped in frustration.

Pearl cried and squirmed as she was drug from the room. Mantodea soldiers quickly marched into the foyer, grabbing Langston by the arms, and made him walk towards the reception room. He watched on as Kinth was forced to exit by him.

"See you soon, stranger," Kinth spoke candidly to Langston as he passed, winking his eye.

"Wait, what? What's going on? Why they leaving?" Langston asked.

"Have a seat," The Guardian stated with his hand extended toward a couch in the room, "Don't worry about them. Let's talk – you and me." The door of the reception room slammed shut, as muffled shouting from Pearl covered the walls of the room.

"First, you threaten to kill me. Then you want to talk. Which is it? Man, all of y'all crazy. This place is crazy. I just want to get out of here. I want to find my way home. I don't really care how I got here anymore. This shit is nuts. I – "

"Quiet! Look, I know who you are, at least I think I do," the Guardian interjected.

Langston looked at the Guardian with disbelief, as he waited for him to elaborate on his statement.

"My father ran this place. He was Hock City's first leader. But he had bad habits. He couldn't control his flesh, and thus, impregnated a bunch of women. And um…I'm just going to be frank here. I had these women removed. See, I couldn't let the good people of Hock City find out about my father's affairs. It would have been a disgrace to Guardian's Grove if his behavior was discovered. It would have ruined us. My family would have been stripped of the Guardian's estate and benefits. You understand? The people here worship this place. You follow what I'm saying? His actions would have downgraded us. We would have had to live out there with the rest of those filthy, retched people. No, no – couldn't let that happen. So, quietly - I did what I had to."

"You son of a bitch."

"No. Son of a weak man, actually. But I took care of that. I had each one these women removed, quietly. I instructed my men to take them to different places - to other corridors."

"How could you harm women? What kind of person are you?" Langston stood to his feet.

"Sit down! *Sit* down!"

Guards approached Langston with their weapons drawn; Langston returned to his seat.

"I didn't hurt anyone. I did these women a favor because my father wasn't going to take care of them. No harm came to them by me. Now, what happens outside of those walls is not my concern."

"Yeah that's what I keep hearing. Nobody cares what happens outside the walls. Bastard. Pregnant women. What kind of a monster are you? And how did you even know for sure? How do you now know this actually happened?"

"A monster? Me? No. All I did was take action against contradictory behavior. And what more proof did I need?" The Guardian laughed at the comments, "To hell with proof. There was enough unanswered questions floating around. Suspicion was all the proof I required."

Langston shook his head and mumbled to himself.

"I did what I knew my brother wouldn't! I had to keep our crest pure! My father – such a weak man. But to most, like my brother - he had no faults – he was perfect in their eyes."

"Sounds like jealousy to me."

"I don't care what it sounds like to you. You don't know what this place was like. You don't know my struggle. To me, it sounds like perfect justice. It sounds like decisiveness, action; an obligatory act to protect -"

"Your status and your greed," Langston interjected.

The Guardian clinched his jaw at Langston's statement.

"Ah, to be so young and stupid. So impressionable."

"This would explain why I don't recognize anything about this city."

"You won't remember anything. More than likely, you were brought into this world in one of the other six corridors. Most people don't travel beyond the walls of their homes. The dangers in that desert is too much for most to bear. How you made it here, unharmed – for the most part - is an amazement."

"I still don't understand."

"What more is there to understand?"

"No one ever told me, anything. About what happened, this place – nothing. And they call me human. I don't have abilities like the people here."

"Yes, yes – I noticed. Seems father enjoyed a variety. I heard about you people. Never thought I would be sitting here speaking to one of you in person.

"So I keep hearing."

"Did you actually think that the world was only as large, as the walls you lived inside of? Pathetic. The world is much larger, kid. Much, much larger. Hock City is one of seven corridors that sit inside Pineville. They all operate differently, and under different leadership. The leaders, at one point, worked together. They developed the tunnels with doorways that bridged our worlds. But some didn't agree to these arrangements, so they created their own tunnels. These tunnels lead to very dark and treacherous places. You were in one of those tunnels, when we captured you. So, you should be thanking me. But the other tunnels were available so that we could travel to different areas safely, and for some discreetly. My father practically built Hock City. But his behavior in the dark wasn't that of a leader. He got around, a lot. We – me, Pearl and Kinth are the only three kids he had legitimately. In the beginning, he kept up with appearances, but he grew careless. He would go missing, neglect business and squander lines. People started to ask questions. So I put a stop to it."

"You killed him, didn't you? Your own father - your own family? What is wrong with you?"

"I did what was required! I didn't just turn a blind eye to his conduct like most. That would have accomplished nothing!"

Langston stared at the floor and shook his head. His anger grew, just as much as the confusion.

"That explains nothing. Why was I in the middle of the desert with a hospital gown on of all things?"

The Guardian poured himself a drink, as he listened to Langston process what he had heard.

"That - my friend - is not for me to figure out. Honestly, I don't really give a shit. But you are here now, brother. Let's celebrate and talk business! You can work for me. We can figure out what we will tell people later. I'm sure people will have questions, like why a human is now inside of our city."

"Brother? I'm not your brother!" Langston lunged at the Guardian, grabbing him by his suit lapel and the collar of his shirt. The grab caused the Guardian to drop the wine bottle, alerting security nearby.

"I will never consider you a brother. Family doesn't do that to family!"

A guard rushes the area before Langston could do the Guardian any harm, striking him in the head. Langston fell to the floor at the feet of his newly discovered sibling. His eyes blurred before he passed out.

"Well, what are you waiting for? Take him downstairs and put him with the others. We will figure out what to do with them shortly." The Guardian looked down at Langston one more time, "Well, what do we have here?"

The Dream

"Come here! Come here, buddy! Oh man, look at you! You are getting big, boy! And looking more and more like your momma. Look at those eyes."

"You need to come see him more often. He will be taller than you next time."

"Ha! He can be as tall as those walls and would still be my little man! Isn't that right, son?"

Langston looked up and smiled.

"I'm serious; you need to come see us more."

"Honey, come on now. We talked about this. You know I am doing the best that I can. You know I love you both."

"Then *prove* it. Stay with me."

"Baby – you know I can't do that. I have to continue this. You know I have a lot going on."

"Everybody got a lot going on. Why? Why does it have to be you?"

Langston played with animal figurines on the floor while he listened to the conversation.

His mother continued, "What about us? What about me? We are your family. You have peace here with us. Look at you! You are greying already. That city, and what you are doing, is driving you mad. You're spreading yourself thin."

"Enough! Please!" the man snapped, startling both Langston and his mother. He grew frustrated with her lecture. He sighed as he shook his head and watched Langston more, while smiling at his presence.

He hesitantly walked over to her. She cried softly in one of her hands, before turning her back to him to continue folding laundry. He kissed her shoulder and then turned her around by her hips. He rubbed her head with his head before kissing her cheek.

"I'm sorry. I will do better with my time; I will figure something out. You know I love you. We have something special. We share something I haven't had with any other - something strong. I will figure out a way so that we won't be apart for long. You know I will do my best."

"I know – I know you will. It's just - it's just – hard. It's lonely without you. I'm tired of doing so much by myself. I'm sorry."

"Don't apologize. You're right. I understand."

The Awakening

"Mr. Langston! Mr. *Langston!*" Jesse screamed and sung his name as loud as he could to wake him. Langston lied on his stomach on the cold cellar floor – breathing but unresponsive.

Déjà vu.

The cellar was divided by rows of large barrels, filled with wine and ale. More bottles of alcohol were found in cubbies, lined on the wall.

Langston, Jesse and Kinth were separated and tied to columns within the different rows.

Kinth listened as Jesse did his best to wake Langston. "You're wasting your breath, kid. He is out. Probably a concussion. Might as well relax, 'cause he may be like that for a while." He scanned the area. "Haven't seen this room in a long time. My father would spend many nights down here, drinking and working at that table over there. Still looks the same way it did the last time I saw him."

In the middle of the room was a large, circular table, just beyond the rows of barrels. It consisted of small stacks of books, and papers, while a globe rested atop of it. These items appeared to have been there for some time, based on the amount of dust and spider webs that rested on top of them. The room itself didn't see many visitors anymore, other than a quick grab-and-go of the various ales and wines stocked.

"Wait a minute. I know your voice. You are the man from the station."

"That would be I."

"I still have a scar from when you threw me out."

"Sorry, kid. You shouldn't have been trespassin.' You think that scar is bad - you should see mine. There are things in that desert that could have done a lot worse. Be happy that I sent you about your business before someone else did."

"Whatever, man. Are you going to help me wake him up or what?"

"Wake him up and then what?"

"Find a way outta here! What else?"

Kinth laughed at the comment.

"C'mon man! You are strong. And you know this place better than anyone else."

"Kid, there is only but so much I can do. There is only one of me and plenty of them. I'm sure they called reinforcements. I know I would have. We are outnumbered."

"We gotta try something. We are smarter than they are."

Kinth reflected on Jesse's words as he continued to look around the room. He remembered the days of his youth when he would run around the cellar with his sister and brother, hiding inside and behind empty barrels.

He also remembered his early adulthood, when his father made him the head of the Grove's Army. His father celebrated the event with dignitaries in the mansion on one day and then again in private with him - in the cellar, giving him his first drink.

You are a man now.

Kinth was made the head of security, not just because he was the Guardian's first-born, but also because he had abilities of which his father was aware, long before Kinth knew of them himself. There were natural leadership and instinctual skills. Skills that his father could sense before the event.

He made Kinth responsible for the safety of Hock City and the immediate areas outside of the wall. There was peace and joy amongst Hock City's citizens when Kinth and his father held their positions. That all changed.

"Hello? *Hello*?" Jesse sang, to regain Kinth's attention.

"All right kid, shut up. Good grief – goin' give me an ulcer."

"Mr. Langston! Mr. *Langston*!" Jesse tried again to wake Langston as Kinth pondered a strategy.

Kinth looked carefully between the barrels to see where Langston was. He came up with an idea that would wake him. He kicked a barrel with one forceful thrust of his leg, knocking it to the floor. The impact caused the barrel to burst into pieces, while the contents covered the area in which Langston lied. The fluid poured fast enough that it rose high enough from the ground to cover Langston's nose, causing him to gasp for air.

He was finally awakened.

Q&A

Langston lifted his head from the floor and looked around, while he gathered his composure. A streak of blood ran down the back of his ear and the side of his neck; his head pulsated.

"What is this place? Where am I?"

"Well, look at who decided to rejoin the land of the living. Did you get enough beauty rest, pretty boy?"

"Mr. Langston! You're awake! Finally!"

"Jesse?"

"Yeah, it's me."

"Oh, good. You're okay. Where are we?" Langston wiped his face and neck with the sleeve of his shirt. He checked his arm; his watch was missing. "Dammit."

"What?"

"He took my watch."

"That's my brother for you. "

"I don't know; looks like a dungeon. Almost like the tunnels. Smells weird down here. Kinda like the alleys in the city."

"This is my father's old cellar."

"Kinth?"

"Yep."

"Our father, the true Guardian?"

"I see my brother briefed you."

"I guess you can say that. Told me a lot of stuff. At first, I thought I was dreaming some of the shit he told me." Langston sat up and rested his back against a barrel, rubbing the back of his head and neck again. "Damn. That asshole hit me hard; wasn't necessary."

The room grew quiet as each one of them looked around the cold, shadowy environment. They were all thinking one thing: how to get out. There was only one set of doors, which were more than likely guarded by the Guardian's security. Getting past them would be a task.

"What else did he tell you?" Kinth asked.

"Man…what the hell is going on in this city? He told me that he killed the original Guardian - our father - and took over. Is this true? Well, actually, he said that he had him 'removed.' I kinda put two and two together."

Kinth grumbled to himself. Then he kicked another barrel, smashing it with ease.

"I don't mean to add to your frustrations. But I really need to know more than what he told me. Anything. A little bit more info can help me figure the rest out myself."

"Wait a minute. Why did you say 'our father?' What did he tell you?"

"He told me that our father impregnated several women - and he said that he had these women removed from the city to protect the family."

"Bullshit!"

"I'm just telling you what he told me."

"I don't believe it. There was no signs of this - never! Not one time has anyone spoken anything like this," Kinth paused his aggravated rant, "I don't want to believe this shit, but let's pretend for a minute that it's true. So, you are trying to tell me that you are a child of one of those women?"

"Seemingly so. Which makes me –"

"My brother." Kinth finished Langston's statement, both of them became silent, as they processed the conversation.

"Whoa," Jesse was stunned by the news.

The room got quiet again. Faint sounds of conversations and footsteps were just outside the doors, along with a subtle blowing of wind that came from cracks in the foundation walls.

"The pretty boy could be my brother. How about that," Kinth chuckled to himself. "I'm not surprised. I knew something was different about you when you came by my station."

"What do you mean?"

"That watch you had on - you remember the design on the face? It's the same design I have on a pin that was given to me."

"What kind of pin?"

"You know, a pin that you put on your clothes. Not a writing pen. When you showed me that watch at the station, it didn't register to me until after that the design was the same."

"Father."

"Yes, he gave you that watch. He gave us all something."

"This pin you speak of, he gave you that too?"

"No, no. It was given to me by someone else."

"Who?"

"I can't say."

Silence filled the space again.

"There you go again. Being cryptic," Langston felt deflated.

"I know. I have no choice in this regard. But I can tell you other things. What's funny is, what my brother told you is probably the first time he has been somewhat honest - ever," Kinth sighed at the brief moment of recollection. "It's tough to talk about the past," he sighed and then continued.

"Yeah, I get it." Langston listened attentively.

"Hock City is just one of many places in the Pines. At one time, this land we walked on was all one. One land, one people – connected; working together toward common goals. Peace, love and survival. We lived in harmony amongst the mountains, the hills and the animals. Many years went by and these people did well. They worked together without much strain or issues. My father, his father, and many generations before them. Then, suddenly, something fell from the sky. Something fell from the stars. Whatever it was - it was large; bigger than any mountain I had ever seen, larger than parts of the sky. It crashed into the ground we walked on, breaking the land. Large cracks, over time grew larger, creating seven separate areas."

"The corridors."

"Right. Whatever this object was - when it fell - it separated our lands. We eventually called the separate areas 'corridors.' This event was devastating. Many of us were torn apart. Our families, way of life – everything. I was very small when this happened and I was changed."

"Changed how?"

"The object from the sky did something to us. The energy within the object combined with the genetics of the people, made us different. It made some of us stronger, smarter, and faster. Shorter, taller, nicer, and meaner. It changed some of us completely. It was like the energy amplified certain things about us. Whatever our individual driving force was, the force that made us live, and hope - this force was amplified. For some, the object killed them on impact. For my father, it made him stronger – like physically strong and wiser. Many people admired his strength. He built many things using mostly his hands and resources from the land. But he was weak when it came to helping others. People took advantage of his kindness."

"The object also brought great evil to this place. More evil than good. When this evilness swept our lands, my father defended those like him; the people who wanted peace. Because of his actions and accomplishments, he was awarded with the title of Guardian, even though he didn't seek this title. He never wanted to lead anyone. He just loved his home - the place he spent his childhood. He just wanted it to be what it once was, before the event. He and many others found a way to connect the lands via the tunnels and bridges. It took many cycles to complete. As the lands moved further apart, my father and others extended the tunnels so that we could always travel to where we needed to go."

"What about me? They call me 'human.' What is a human? And the Desert Dwellers and the other odd looking people?"

"Before the event, everyone on this land were humans. But after the event, most of us were changed. Only a small number of people did not change. These specific people were later considered different. They were outcast by those who were envious of them. The humans scattered and hid all over the seven corridors, blending in and pretending to be different. Others weren't fortunate. They were killed as soon as they were discovered. You are the first I have seen in a while. I am shocked you are still alive."

The energy within the object also affected animals. Many are now able to walk and talk like humans. For some of us, it combined our energies, causing us to have a blend of traits and abilities of other species. The object from the sky crushed others, driving their souls into the land, and I guess this is where the Desert Dwellers come from. Angry, lost souls – whom were trapped in the sand."

Langston closed his eyes as he listened, imagining what the event might have looked like. He envisioned a large ball of light, dark-orange in color, falling from afar. The object appeared tiny in the sky, but grew larger the more he stood and watched it. Eventually, it became large enough where more people stood in wonder to look at it. They held their hands to their faces to provide shade to their eyes - due to its brightness. Soon, these people started to scatter as they became more afraid of the unknown. What was the object and what harm could it do? They ran to their homes and watched from the windows. Then, the sky went dark, after a loud sound traveled across the land.

"I'm at a loss for words."

"It was spectacular and a horrific thing to witness. So I was told. All those people that you have seen, survived that event; or were born after."

"You said you were small when this happened. How did this event affect you?"

"It gave me abilities."

"Which are?"

"I don't know. I was young, so even after the change I felt the same. But the older I got, the more I felt different. All I know is I am stronger than most. Sometimes I have trouble controlling my strength. Other times, I feel strange when I am around people. I know things about them. I have visions, but most of the time the visions are incomplete and sporadic. I don't know what they mean."

"And the sun cycles; what are those?"

"My father told me that before the object fell from the sky, every day had sunlight; every night had darkness. But after the event, the sun would retreat at times, and it would be darkness across the lands. Sometimes it would retreat for a few hours - a few days. Sometimes months. We don't know understand why it does this; it's never the same length of time. When the sun appears, we call it a 'cycle.' During these sun cycles is the only time when you can safely scavenge for resources like food, water or clothing - without much worry of what lurked when darkness came. Darkness in the desert is not safe for anyone. As you know well enough by now."

"So what do you do when its darkness for a long period of time?"

"What else can we do? We survive somehow. Many of us starve or die due to dehydration. Some try to make it to other corridors, even in the midst of the dark. Most don't return."

Unwelcoming Territory

A noise could be heard outside the walls as Kinth explained more about the event that changed the Pines. At first, it was a challenge to gauge from where the sound was coming.

"You hear that?"

"Yep, doesn't sound good," Kinth replied.

"Jesse, wake up! Wake up, Jesse!"

The sound continued; it grew louder and intrusive.

"What is that?" Jesse asked, as he yawned and stretched.

"Sounds like it's coming from that wall."

Kinth, without much effort, broke the chain to which he was confined while walking over to Langston.

"Damn, are you serious? All this time you could have freed us and you just sat there?"

Kinth ignored Langston's complaint as he broke his chains and then did the same for Jesse. The two of them walked closer to the area from which the sound was coming from.

Langston put his head to the cold, dingy wall, as Jesse waited by the column to which he had been attached.

"I'm going to watch from over here, 'cause that don't sound good."

The rumbling behind the wall continued, causing the dim lighting in the room to flicker.

"Watch out," Kinth pushed Langston out of his way just before he threw multiple jabs at the wall. The stones began to shatter, falling to the floor with each punch. A thick layer of dirt started to show, as Kinth destroyed enough of the stones to create an opening.

The three of them stood still as they watched the dirt move. Something from the other side was pushing it.

"Step back," Langston insisted.

Mounds of dirt fell to the floor after moving from the wall. A voice could be heard. A nose burst through the remaining pack of gravel and stone without notice. The nostrils sniffed the room as claws began to show.

"Hey kid, ya' miss me?!"

"Miles!"

"The one and only."

Jesse greeted his friend with a big hug.

"Man, you're dirty!"

"What did you expect? Okay, okay - get off me. Enough with the mushy stuff."

"Man - am I glad to see you!"

"I bet you are." Miles turned to Langston, "Still like staring, I see. You humans, I tell ya.' Nobody told you that staring is rude, sir?"

"Still getting acclimated to things here."

"Well, well – look who decided to come home."

"Good to see you, old friend," Kinth replied.

"Wait, you know Miles?" asked Jesse.

"He was affected by the object from the sky, wasn't he?" Langston interjected.

"I sure was, human. I was a friend of Hock City's first and only Guardian. God rest his soul. Not that new jerk – no offense Kinth. Before the event, when that freakin' thing fell from the sky, I was just an annoying mole that ate everything in the Guardian's garden. After it hit, it did something to me. I started to understand you humans. Soon, I learned how to speak. After a while, the Guardian and I became friends. My companions and I helped him create the tunnels."

As Miles spoke, more of his kind dropped into the room behind him.

"Anyway. Let me introduce y'all. Everybody, this is my family. Family – this is everybody. I heard that the Guardian's goons got to ya,' and brought you here. Couldn't figure out where you were at first. We had to circle around a couple times until we were able to get your scent. We could smell the human before you two."

"Of course you could," Langston spoke under his breath.

"Your scent came from above ground for a while. We couldn't risk being seen, so we stayed below, and waited for an opportunity. We got lucky when they brought you down here. Oh, and thanks for making that hole - by the way. Would have taken us forever to get through that concrete."

"Anytime," Kinth said.

"We dug a route to the nearest tunnel that will lead you out. The city is a mad house after that scene you two caused, so we can't go that way. That prick-of-a-brother of yours shut down all access points. He closed all the gates and forced most of the people outside the walls. He is killing anyone who saw the human."

"Damn, all those people," replied Langston.

"Yep. It's his way to keep this quiet and flush out any more of you."

"We need to go! They will come for us soon!"

"Hold on kid. We have a couple problems, though."

"What problems?" Kinth asked.

"First of all, we aren't sure which corridor we dug to. We run the risk of going to an unwelcoming territory. And two, the tunnel we dug will only fit the human and anybody smaller."

"Wait, unwelcoming territory? I thought that event just divided the land," Langston interrupted.

"Yes! But it divided people's hearts and minds too! You really think everyone was going to stay the same after losing loved ones, land and other things that were important to them? For a while it was every man for himself out here. Killing and more killing. Madness. No unity. This was something else my father fought against. He worked hard to prevent wars between the lands."

All eyes were on Kinth at this moment. His words shook the room because of his extraordinary size and passion.

"Relax people. Let's get back on track. Kinth, you are not going to be able to fit in the tunnels we dug. It's as simple as that. But we can circle back and widen it. This will take some time, though."

"Understood. No sense in wasting time. Go on without me. I can manage." Kinth began to gather the chains to which they were once attached to, combining them to create a weapon using only the links. "I have things to settle here anyway. We will meet again."

Langston walked over to Kinth, and extended his hand. They shook as brothers whom were once strangers.

"Hey kid, take care of him, will ya'?"

"I got him covered," Jesse replied with a cocky tone, as he wasted no time entering the tunnel behind Miles.

"Goodness, the theatrics in this place. All right kid, let's go."

Langston started to climb into the hole after Jesse, when he stopped suddenly. "Wait. What are you going to do to him?"

"Don't worry about it. My problem."

"No, it's *our* problem."

"Oh, so all of a sudden you are a part of this? It's *my* problem. Go home - live your life. Maybe our paths will cross again."

"Oh boy. The drama! Can we go please?" Miles grew frustrated.

"Why wouldn't I be a part? I just found out that we are brothers of the same father. I won't have much of a life without knowing how this ends."

"We need to go, now. I can smell someone headed toward this room," Miles chimed in.

"Okay, tough guy. What do you suggest then?" Kinth asked.

"Find a way out - meet us at your station."

"Can't go back there."

"Right, they will check there first. Okay, well find us somehow; send us a signal. Just deal with him later. He is the only one who knows what happened to our father. If you kill him then you kill information we need. Besides, he will be obsessed with finding you, now that he knows you are alive. Have him come to us, on our terms. You are strong - yes — but you are stronger with us at your sides. I can help somehow."

Kinth sat down on a barrel of ale, and stroked his beard; he listened to Langston's offer.

"Go, now. I will find you."

"But —"

"Go!"

The doors in the room opened, moments after Kinth shoved Langston into the tunnel. He moved a few barrels of ale in front of the hole to block the entrance. Then he pretended to be bound to the column that he had been before.

"Ah, my brother Kinth," the Guardian looked around as he spoke. "Wait. Wait a minute. I told you to bring them all to the cellar!"

"We did, sir."

"Well, where are they? Find them!"

"They are long gone. Out of your reach, *brother*."

"Nothing is out of my reach."